Other Books By Velma Crow

THE LAZARUS GENERATION – COME FORTH
The Death, Burial, and Resurrection of Your Dreams

…will reignite the flame of desire and guide you to the full establishment of your divine call. Through teaching and self-examination exercises at the end of each chapter, this book will enable you to believe again, stretch forth your withered dream, and prophesy to the dry bones.

SPIRIT WINDS
Psalms from the Secret Place
Volume One

Sometimes my heart—my spirit sings, sometimes angels sing,
at other times the Spirit and the Lord sing.
Drawn from experiences in the supernatural.

PORTALS, REALMS, AND REVELATIONS
Volume One
A Spiritual House

During times of refreshing the Lord showed me the building of my spiritual house—His plan for my life. This volume contains various encounters in the presence of the Lord and the revelation, inner healing, and/or deliverance I received during each visit.

REVELATION

OF

VISITATION

REVELATION

OF

VISITATION

A BASIC GUIDE
TO DEVELOPING A
<u>NATURALLY SUPERNATURAL</u>
RELATIONSHIP
WITH THE LIVING GOD

Velma Crow

TMN/Wisdom Merchants Publishing

Revelation of Visitation
A Basic Guide To Developing A Naturally Supernatural Relationship
With The Living God
Copyright © 2008

Scriptures, unless otherwise noted, are taken from THE AMPLIFIED BIBLE, Old Testament copyright © 1965, 1987 by the Zondervan Corporation. The Amplified New Testament copyright © 1958, 1987 by the Lockman Foundation. Parentheses ( ) signify additional phases of meaning included in the original word, phrase, or clause of the original language. Brackets [ ] contain justified clarifying words or comments not actually expressed in the immediate original text, as well as definitions of Hebrew and Greek names.

All quotes from the King James Version are taken from software published by Candlelight Publishing, Mesa, AZ. (c) 1993 by Infobases, Inc. and © 1993 by Eagle Computing.

Unless otherwise indicated, all word definitions and word studies are taken from the Strong's Hebrew and Greek Lexicon on software published by Candlelight Publishing, Mesa, AZ., © 1993 by Infobases, Inc. and ©1993 by Eagle Computing.
KJV—*King James Version*, Authorized King James Version

All emphasis added to Scripture are at the discretion of the author. TMN/Wisdom Merchants Publishing style capitalizes nouns and pronouns that refer to God, Lord, Holy Spirit, Father and/or Son. Also note we choose to not capitalize the name satan and/or various related terms signifying his name.

Cover Design Copyright © 2009
Velma Crow
Protected by United States and International Copyright Laws
TMN/Wisdom Merchants
admin@wisdommerchants.org
First Edition 2006
Second Edition 2013
ISBN-13: 978-0615804590
ISBN-10: 0615804594

ACKNOWLEDGEMENTS

My deep appreciation extends to Frances McDannel Spiller, Diana Meyer, Penny Hansen, Carol Doddridge, Sandra Martin, Sherry Bidison and Lois Barrett who have trusted me to share some of their experiences with you in this book. A special thank you to all the men, women and children who have allowed me to plant the seeds of possibilities for relationship with a living God in their hearts.

Thank you my brothers and sisters in Illinois, Texas, and Oregon, for allowing me to pour into your souls. Thank you for encouraging and supporting me during the development of this teaching. May you continue hungering and thirsting for His presence, for His Word. and for righteousness. May you continue multiplying as you pour into others, thereby establishing the Kingdom of Heaven wherever you go.

A special "Thank You" to Pastors David and Barbara Vaughan. You accepted me even before you knew me. You loved me when I was unlovable. At our first meeting, you began caring for me, embracing me as family, binding up my wounds with freely given unconditional love. You drew me out of my self-imposed tomb of aloneness. You recognized and honored the gift of God in me. I love you both and will forever be grateful.

Roxanne Sprout and Kathy Wilson
Thank you for jumping in as emergency proofer and editor.
Your time was invaluable to me.
"Thank you" doesn't begin to express my gratitude.

DEDICATION

This book is dedicated to:
Betty Martin and Marjory Root
Sisters
Life-long Christians
Who in their golden years
Through this teaching, discovered
True, personal relationship with their Lord and
Fell in love with
JESUS CHRIST,
The Lover of Their Souls

SPECIAL DEDICATION

Frances McDannel Spiller

Your dedication to my success portrays a
greater love than I have known.
I know had it not been for the love of God
shed abroad in your heart it would have been
impossible
for you to make the sacrifices you made
on my behalf.
Thank you for your
relentless dedication
to do all you can to see that
I walk in the fullness of my call.
I also know the sacrifices you make are not just for me
but for everyone who will be touched though my ministry.

TABLE OF CONTENTS

FIRST THINGS FIRST

SOUL TRAVEL
versus
SPIRIT LED ENCOUNTERS

In pursuit of a relationship with God, there may come a time you desire to experience the supernatural realm. This is a good desire. However, if you decide to take matters into your own hands, you will most likely end up in the domain of darkness. This is satan's domain, populated by demons of various rank and order. Should you make this choice having a soulish experience with the demonic realm rather than a Throne Room experience with God. You have just set yourself up with an open door for demons to take advantage of you and do mischief through you though you may be convinced you are doing good or just having fun. Yes, this is true even for Christians who decide to allow their soul to be their god rather than yielding to the Spirit of God within them. You are deceived into thinking this acceptable.

There are many differences between soul travel and being led of—caught up by the Spirit of God. Let's look at some of the differences.

1

SOUL TRAVEL

(Soul travel may also be called shape-shifting, channeling, transcendental meditation, being led by spirit guides, and various other things.)

If you are successful in entering the supernatural realm via your soul, you have violated the blood covering of salvation and exposed yourself to manipulation, confusion, deception, delusion, and a very strong possibility of becoming demon infested. The demons may give you a feeling of power and authority, but **it is all false, a snare to your soul**. What actually happens if you continue this type "visitation" is, you will be operating under the influence of demonic control, the quality of your life will deteriorate.

The fruit of the demonic realm is tainted. Check yourself with the following list. Repent each time you recognize your attitude or condition. (This is not a complete list but repenting through it will get you back on the right track.)

- You have entered the demonic realm thereby giving demons access to your soul.
- Your personality begins being affected—little by little at first, then your family and friends begin noticing the differences in your personality.
- The demons in you invite others to join them in their new domain—YOU!
- They continue becoming more and more deeply entrenched in your soul.
- You begin living in a cloud of darkness that you carry with you wherever you go and the atmosphere surrounding you is adversely affected by that darkness.

- You give demons a type of transportation that takes them places they would never have opportunity to go to do mischief to people they would have no other way to touch.
- You become calculating, distrustful, full of pride, angry, suspicious, bitter, reclusive, etc.
- The negative traits of godlessness are reflected in your personality.
- You begin avoiding the light of truth, love, goodness, and kindness—starving your soul of life and hope.
- You become isolated especially from godly influence.
- The less godly influence the more the demonic gain control.
- You realize you are doing things you have judged others for doing.
- The once random ungodly thoughts capture your mind more often and keep it longer, choking out godly attributes.
- You realize you are doing things you would normally not consider doing.
- Your body becomes filled with the rotten issues of the fruit of negative thoughts and attitudes.
- Dis-ease of your soul develops disease in your body.
- You develop physical—often debilitating illnesses.
- At the very least you are in danger of spending eternity in outer darkness [Matthew 8:17].

Soul travel is very dangerous.

- If something prevents your soul from returning to your body, your body will die.

The only way out is repentance.
Cry out to God for forgiveness and deliverance.
Don't stop crying out until you are free.
When we confess our sins He is faithful and just to forgive us our sins and cleanse us from all unrighteousness [1 John 1:9].

3

Pray This Prayer:

Father, Your Word says when we confess our sins
You are faithful and just to forgive us and cleanse us of all
unrighteousness.
I confess as sin that I have taken a wrong road and have opened
myself to demonic oppression.
I confess the sin of playing god, trying to do in the flesh things that
can only be done by and through Your Spirit.
I renounce the works of darkness and of the flesh.
I confess I have trespassed against the Blood of the Jesus.
Deliver me from the power of darkness and
of the wickedness that has invaded me.
Restore my soul by the cleansing power of the
Blood of Your Son shed on the Cross.
Help me set my feet on the path of righteousness.
I ask all of this in the name of Jesus Christ
And I yield to His Lordship over my life.

Now, RUN to the Throne of Grace.

*   *   *

TO BE LED OR CAUGHT UP BY THE SPIRIT OF GOD

If you are a Christian, the Spirit of God dwells in you and is your guide. Your sins are covered by the Blood of Jesus and you are protected by angelic hosts. You will most likely experience inner healing and deliverance. You may have encounters with angels, and with Father, Son, and Holy Spirit. You are given revelation along with the wisdom, knowledge and understanding to interpret what you see. You can be used to do good and accomplish things in ways you can't with "natural" skills and talents or through "the soulish realm."

Being led or caught up by the Spirit of God is an experience of your spirit communing with Holy Spirit. These experiences may be limited to the Spirit realm but often occur in and affect the natural. You may be conveyed by the Spirit to other places on earth or even into the heavenlies to intervene in various situations including in individual lives. These experiences can and often do result in physical translation as happened often to Elijah and as Phillip the Deacon was after baptizing the Ethiopian eunuch. This is sometimes referred to as being transported.

- As you yield to the Spirit of God in you, your soulish power diminishes; God reigns!
- In this state, you can be used to confront demons and tear down strongholds and thrones of iniquity in your bloodline, your city, wherever you are appointed by God.
- Your personality is changed—your soul becomes peaceful—your heart passionate about the things of God.
- You start wanting what He wants and doing what you see Him do—saying what you hear Him say.
- Your discernment is increased to distinguish between what is holy and what is profane.
- You are equipped to destroy the works of the devil as Jesus did and still does, through us.
- You gain the mind of Christ and begin learning the ways of God.
- The atmosphere changes wherever you are; peace increases and light reigns.
- The glory of God is perceived—even seen on you— demons tremble.
- You carry and establish the Kingdom wherever you go just as Peter did when the glory cloud overshadowed people and they were healed The shadow that healed was actually the "shadow" of the glory of God.
- The fruit and gifts of the Spirit become evident in your life.

This type of spiritual transforming experience is increasing among God's people today.

The _purpose_ of Visitation is
To develop
awareness of Habitation

- The _outgrowth_ of visitation should include:
  - Inner Healing.
  - Deliverance.
  - Spiritual Growth.
  - Deeper Relationship with the triune God.
  - The Establishment of the Kingdom of Heaven around us.
- When we walk down the street people should be able to recognize that the Kingdom of Heaven has come near.
- The atmosphere should change when we walk into a room.
- We should begin bearing the fruit of the Kingdom of God:
  - Our lives reflecting Jesus
    - Salvations, signs, wonders and miracles manifesting everywhere we go.

Old Testament prophets are examples of _Visitation_.

Jesus is our example of _Habitation_.

INTRODUCTION

RENEWAL

Though I had been experiencing visitations for years, both angelic and with the Lord, I had become distracted by the duties of ministry and family. For months I had neglected those times to pull aside with no agenda, no need, no question, simply to be with my Lord.

On December 23, 2005, the voice of an angelic messenger woke me saying, "And the Lord would say. . ."

"Wait a minute!" I say jumping out of bed. "I need to get a pen and some paper." Normally I keep these things by my bed but yesterday I had taken my notebook to my computer to do some transcription in the living room and failed to return it. Back in bed, pen and paper in hand, pillows stacked against the headboard, I say, "Okay. I'm ready."

The angel begins again:

"And the Lord would say, 'Come again to Me. Draw near to Me for I miss you and I long for your presence.'"

His words pierce my heart. I have been longing for the presence of my Lord, but have allowed my life to become so cluttered I have not taken the time to pull aside to meet with Him in the Secret Place.

"Lord, I don't remember the way." Tears stream from my eyes. As soon as I respond to the angelic messenger, the Lord responds to me.

"The way is clear. The path is well lighted. Just follow My footprints left on the path when I have come to you. (I looked and saw luminous footprints where the Lord had walked.) I came to you while you slept. I watched you and breathed My love over you, for your eyes were heavy and your soul unaware of My presence. (Even as I write His words my mind begins reaching into my day.) Practice My presence again. Have you forgotten the sweetness of our time together? Do not let the world nor your assignment come between us. You cannot go on alone. You have put a barrier between your heart and mine."

Immediately I see a situation I had experienced. It was like a page from my history, a living page standing between my Lord and me. I realized I had stood it there as a shield so I wouldn't look past it to a place where I felt He might not protect me from the hurt of it. I had never before shielded myself from Him, Although as a child I had run from the inexplicable atmosphere of His manifest presence. My parents, though devoted to Him, did not understand an actual experience with Him. The presence of His Spirit was not a recognized part of their lives. As I matured, I learned to run to Him, bury my face in His chest and press into His arms. Even when the deepest hurts were crushing my soul, He has always been my refuge! Why now, would I put anything between us?

"Forgive me, Lord! How could I not have known? How could I have grown so cold toward you? I know you've been with me, still working on my soul, transforming me, healing me, restoring me. How could I be so complacent?"

"You know the way. Allow your heart to reach for Me again. Draw near to Me for I am near, waiting, yes, longing to embrace you."

Now He is standing in front of me. I fall into His arms. Tears of relief fill my eyes. How could I have neglected allowing Him to hold me? He came seeking me out as a lost sheep! Though my life is spent in pursuit of my assignment, I had neglected the Master's presence! How could I?

He's still holding me, so passionately yet, so gently. HE CAME FOR ME! Tears flood my eyes again. I have become satisfied with His shadow, the mere remembrance of Him!

"You know the way. Set your feet on the familiar path. (My feet begin sensing the warmth of the path though they have not yet touched it.) As you come, I will cause your eyes to be opened so you will see things along the way you have not noticed before. The path is well lighted; you will not stumble nor falter."

The path begins singing to me:

Come.
You know the way.
The way of rest.
The way of refreshing.
Come
Let your feet be as hinds feet
As I carry you along
Into the arms
Of the One True Love.

The voice is sweet, familiar, comforting—it is the voice of Holy Spirit. I see the face of The Path with eyes full of acceptance and assurance, drawing me to follow. My feet hunger to feel The

Path beneath them. As I yield to The Path, I begin running.

The surroundings near The Path, though barren here, quickly give way to a lush forest. (In my youth I would go into the woods and sit, leaning against a tree near a pond. I would sing and quote scriptures, not knowing I was communing with the Lord until I felt His presence approaching, then I would run home, frightened, unfamiliar with the feelings His presence stirred in my soul.) Now I run to Him.

He's standing, waiting for me just inside the parameter of the woods. His right hand is extended to me. I'm amazed as I realize that even though we are under a canopy of various leafy trees there is no shadow, the light of His glory overcomes all darkness. The brilliance of His white garment catches my eyes but they are hungry for His face. I feel His eyes searching my face and look up to Him.

"Where would I go without you?" Is that my heart or His? Then The Voice of Many Waters blesses my soul:

"I will never leave you. I cannot forsake you. You are part of Me. We are one. Abide in Me. Do not be satisfied by a touch to the fringe of My garment. I am not satisfied with a timid touch required only to fill a need. I long for you to cling to Me joyfully. I long for you to require soul satisfaction that comes only with your entire being engulfed in My full presence, a living connection with My being, not a quick touch of My garment. I am here for you, ever present with you.

"Please do not ignore Me for I am not complete without you, nor can you survive without Me. In Me, you are ROBUST and full of life. Apart from Me you grow empty and cold. Choose Life. Choose Me rather than the distractions of your life and assignment. We will fulfill the assignment together if you will but walk with Me."

"LORD! I will! I will draw near! I will hear the whisperings of Your heart. I will stay. I will remain hidden in You. Touching Your garment does not fill my heart with the joy of Your very presence. Flood my soul with You, Lord, as I am renewed in Your presence."

The clock in the tower a few blocks from my window chimes the hour. *How can I leave this place?*

"The duties of the day are calling. Let's walk through this day together you and Me—walking as one."

"Oh, Yes Lord!"

"You know, it is possible to remain in My presence as you proceed through your day. At various times pull aside and reaffirm yourself in Me so you will be filled with strength to finish the tasks. As you do this, the Kingdom will begin forming around you. Keep your mind stayed—anchored in Me."

* * * * * * * *

This visitation began a new era in my life, an era of daily, purposely meeting with the Lord, giving Him my full attention—not in study nor in prayer and meditation, rather as one would spend time with a spouse or close friend.

In the spring of 2006, the Lord showed me a friend's "spiritual house" and said I was to take her there when she was ready. That was such an exciting experience! After she left my apartment as I celebrated and rejoiced in His goodness, the Lord spoke to me again. "Now, I want you to bring many, many others to Me, here in this place."

Bringing my friends, their friends, and many others to Him

in this place of manifest presence, watching them be healed and transformed as they commune with Him, one-on-one, face-to-face, quickly became one of the most fulfilling aspects of my assignment.

This book contains scriptural references, accounts, and foundational teachings that will dispel fear, ease discomfort of the unknown, and assuage unbelief so others can understand the biblical precedents of relationship between the Living God and mankind.

If you will permit Him, He will reveal mysteries of His Kingdom and show you unspeakable things, sights you could not imagine in your wildest dreams. In the process, He will heal you of hindering memories, wounds, misbeliefs, and any other irregularities in your soul that could keep you from lovership with Him. He will unlock doors you don't even know you have and lovingly shine the light of salvation (wholeness) into every dark or crippled area. He will restore your soul. You will truly be made whole in Him and find the peace that surpasses all understanding.

* * * * * * * * *

Many of us desire a deeper relationship with God, Father, Son and Holy Spirit, but just don't know how to get there. Often we don't know exactly what we mean when we say, "I want more of You, Lord." We want to experience the Kingdom of Heaven but haven't a clue where to find the gate, let alone how to step through it.

If you have entertained such thoughts, this book was written with you in mind. I'll take you through scriptures of such experiences to lay a solid, biblical foundation. I'll share with you some of my own experiences as well as experiences of other people for whom I have been privileged to be the vessel Holy

Spirit poured through to lead into this awesome naturally supernatural life. He desires to make His abode, His special dwelling place, IN US ^{John 14:23}! But, the door opens from the inside. He tells us in Revelation 3:20:

> *Behold, I stand at the door and knock; if anyone hears and listens to and heeds My voice and opens the door, I will come in to him and will eat with him, and he will eat with Me.*

He truly desires to come in. We have to open the door. Guess what! When He comes in, He doesn't just sit inside silently. He doesn't just talk to us when we decide to pray. Unfortunately, when He speaks, we often don't hear or we think it's just our own thoughts. However, He promises us in John 10, verse 27:

> *The Sheep that are My own hear and are listening to My voice; and I know them, and they follow me.*

Just as surely as He spoke in ages past He still speaks today, and not only guides us, but as His Word lives in us it begins changing us so that our desires become what He desires for us. Our ways begin aligning with His ways. The kingdoms of our heart become transformed to His Kingdom. Often these changes are subtle. So subtle, in fact, we normally don't even perceive we are changing until we suddenly realize we don't do the things we used to do. We don't think or talk the way we used to think and talk. Our priorities have changed and we have truly become new men and women, new creatures in Christ.

> *Therefore if any person is [engrafted] in Christ, the Messiah, he is a new creation, (a new creature altogether); the old [previous moral and spiritual condition] has passed away. Behold the fresh and new has come* ^{2 Corinthians 5:17}.

For neither is circumcision [now] of any importance, nor uncircumcision, but [only] a new creation, [the result of a new birth and a new nature in Christ Jesus, the Messiah]
Galatians 6:15

Now, the word "creation" here actually does mean creature, creation and several other things including "the act of founding, establishing, building," etc. We are being built into a house, a temple, a sanctuary, a dwelling place for the Creator of the universe!

Do you not know that your body is the temple, the very sanctuary of the Holy Spirit Who lives within you, Whom you have received as a gift from God? You are not your own 1 Corinthians 6:19.

Another interesting thing about the word translated "creature" is that it is from a root word which means "to make habitable to people, a place, region, island; hence to found a city, colony, state; to create: of God creating the worlds; to form, shape, i.e., to completely change or transform." Any way we look at it, God wants to transform us into a new habitation. He has already paid the price for the renovation!

You were bought with a price, purchased with a preciousness and paid for, made His own. So then, honor God and bring glory to Him in your body. 1 Corinthians 6:20.

The first mention of "habitation" in the Scriptures is found in Exodus 15:2: *The LORD is my strength and song, and He is become my salvation: He is my God, and I will prepare Him an habitation; my father's God, and I will exalt him.* (KJV) Here "habitation" is translated from the Hebrew word, "navah" and is a verb meaning "to beautify or adorn."

As we all know, *He inhabits the praises of Israel* Psalms 22:3.

In this instance to inhabit means "to make a dwelling place."

Habitation is more than just living in a particular place. Inhabiting a place involves making that place comfortable and accommodating and affecting the surrounding area as well. He makes His abode (special dwelling place—habitation) in us and when He does, our atmosphere changes. People notice there has been a change or changes in us. God is living within!

Communication with the Living God is one of the greatest gifts ever given to mankind. Everyone living in the same house must communicate in some way. As we communicate with the Spirit of the Living God, He beautifies and adorns us as He transforms us to reflect Christ ^{Galatians 4:19}. We even carry a new aroma, the *fragrance of the knowledge of Christ.*

> *But thanks be to God, Who in Christ always leads us in triumph as trophies of Christ's victory and through us spreads and makes evident the fragrance of the knowledge of God everywhere,* ***For we are the sweet fragrance of Christ which exhales unto God****, discernible alike among those who are being saved and among those who are perishing: To the latter it is an aroma wafted from death [a fatal odor, the smell of doom];* ***to the former it is an aroma from life to life [a vital fragrance, living and fresh]*** ^{2 Corinthians 2:14-16}.

> *Jesus answered, "If a person [really] loves Me, he will keep My word [obey My teaching]; and My Father will love him, and We will come to him and make our home (abode, special dwelling place, mansion) with him* ^{John 14:23}.

"Keep His Word"—Communication. The more we communicate with Him, the more of His Word we know and practice, the greater the depth of our knowledge of Him will be. His Word (His Love) begins coming alive in us and through us to other people. The fragrance we carry is determined by our relationship with Him.

- If you desire a one-on-one, face-to-face relationship with the living, almighty God;
- If you hunger, as I do, to be a friend of God—even an intimate companion with Him;
- If you want to walk as Enoch, Elijah and various others walked . . .

Then, I invite you to enter into the pages of this book securing that scriptural foundation so that as you journey into the unfathomable mysteries of the Kingdom of God you will be:

- Firm in your faith
- Sure of your foundation
- Having no fear of the enemy, or your flesh misleading you or drawing you into error telling you:
  o It's not right
  o You can't do it
  o Who do you think you are?

Some people refer to this type of spiritual experience as ascending. For me, ascension can be a part of it but there is more. Some people call it visions or open visions. For me, it is more than a vision because I become forever changed with each visitation. For me it is an experience that needs to become a lifestyle as natural to us as breathing. We need to come to the place where visitation becomes habitation and habitation becomes our natural life style—living all the implications of John 17, establishing the Kingdom of heaven around us as we become a living force for change in the Earth.

****

QUESTIONS and EXERCISES

1. Think back over your life. Are there times when you or someone you know, had a dream or vision that seemed too real to be—just a dream?
   a. Jot down a few notes about those times that come to your mind.
   b. Pray about the things you remember and ask the Lord to give you revelation concerning them.
2. Ask the Lord to reveal Himself to and draw you into deeper revelation and relationship.

*   *   *

HABAKKUK 2:2-3

And the Lord answered me and said, Write the vision and engrave it so plainly upon tablets that everyone who passes may [be able to] read [it easily and quickly] as he hastens by. For the vision is yet for an appointed time and it hastens to the end [fulfillment]: it will not deceive or disappoint. Though it tarry, wait [earnestly] for it, because it will surely come; it will not be behindhand on its appointed day.

REVELATION 4:1

After this I looked, and behold, a door standing open in heaven! And the first voice which I had heard addressing me like [the calling of] a war trumpet said, Come up here, and I will show you what must take place in the future. And at once I came under the [Holy] Spirit's power, and behold. A throne stood in heaven, with One seated on the throne!

REVELATION 22:16-17

I, Jesus, have sent My messenger (angel) to you to witness and to give you assurance of these things for the churches (assemblies). I am the Root (the Source) and the Offspring of David, the radiant and brilliant Morning Star.
The Holy Spirit and the bride (the church, the true Christians) say, Come! And let him who is listening say, Come! And let everyone come who is thirsty [who is painfully conscious of his need of those things by which the soul is refreshed, supported, and strengthened]; and whoever [earnestly] desires to do it, let him come, take, appropriate, and drink the water of Life without cost.

*   *   *

FANTASY
versus
IMAGINATION

"Christianity devoid of the supernatural
is just another religion!" Sid Roth

It could be said that the first thing God revealed; about Himself was imagination. He used His imagination to create the universe and mankind. When He developed our solar system, He had mankind in mind to inhabit and have dominion over the third planet from the sun, Earth. Earth had to be surrounded by the universe to maintain the atmospheric conditions which sustain life.

- Everything He did was purposeful with an expected end.
- You can only see the end or result of a thing by imagination.
  - Even though God is outside time and not restricted by the boundaries of it, still He saw and declared the end from the beginning:
    - *[Earnestly] remember the former things which I did of old; for I am God, and there is none like Me. Declaring the end and the result from the beginning, and from ancient times the things that are not yet done saying, My counsel shall stand*

and I will do all My pleasure and purpose ^{Isaiah}
46:9-10

- He created time with understanding and made plans
  to execute certain things during specific periods to
  fulfill His purpose. He says in verse 11, . . . *I have
  spoken, and I will bring it to pass; I have purposed
  it, and I will do it.*

Here's an easy test to discern between fantasy and
imagination. Ask yourself:

- Does it increase my knowledge of God? Imagination will.
- Does it decrease my awareness of God and interfere with
  my knowledge/discernment of right and wrong? Fantasy
  will.

FANTASY:

When God created mankind, Adam, then Eve, they walked
and talked with Him. They communed with Him. They didn't just
hear Him, but saw Him as well. From the first bite of the forbidden
fruit, Eve's soul and fleshly senses were engaged. This is actually
when fantasy was birthed in the Earth. Mankind became "self"
conscious or soulish in lieu of "God" conscious which is
"spiritually minded." From this point on, mankind (except for a
handful of exceptional human beings) could no longer see God
with the natural eye.

Let's examine the serpent's method and motive:

*The serpent said to the woman, You shall not surely die,
for God knows that in the day you eat of it your eyes will
be opened, and you will be like God, knowing the
difference between good and evil and blessing and
calamity.*

*And when the woman saw that the tree was good (suitable
and pleasant) for food and that it was delightful to look*

20

at, and a tree to be desired in order to make one wise, she took of its fruit and ate; and she gave some also to her husband and he ate ^{Genesis 3:4-6}.

You see, satan's invitation to Eve was not just to try something new. His full intent was to engage and activate her soulish desires, tantalize her flesh. Of course right away she gave Adam a bite and suddenly their entire outlook changed. They saw their own nakedness—God's Glory covering was gone. The promise to know good and evil was real. They knew calamity had come into their world.

The first result of their new insight was shame ^{Genesis 3:7}. Shame—one of the most crippling things that can ever happen to the human soul. Shame introduced fear. Shame has a voice that says, "I'm not like Him, therefore He won't want to talk to me!" Fear's voice says, "He can see my ugliness. He knows I'm not worthy to come into His presence."

This is what fantasy is and how it works to separate us from the Love of God. Fantasy does not commune with God. Fantasy communes with our soul and the devil. Fantasy always activates the pleasure system of our flesh. If our inclination is toward sensual things, fantasy can enable us to commit adultery all by ourselves ^{Matthew 5:28}. If we are inclined toward violence, fantasy makes us believe everyone is against us and out to get us so we "take them on" before they have a chance to get us. Some people have ruined their marriage, crushed their families and initiated generations of brokenness by fantasizing about sexual encounters outside their marriage. Others have even cancelled their destinies and affected destinies of other people because they live in a world of fantasy rather than stepping into their divine purpose. The darker our fantasies become, the more harm we do to ourselves and to others.

Fantasy communes with the devil opening us up to become his puppets. Some people, especially addicted to fear and fright purposely engage him, not knowing he will pull them down to hell. This process can begin with playing simple games. However, the devil isn't playing. He has just hooked your soul with that ouija board or some other harmless looking game about witches and demons, magic spells and such.

His next step is to stick his foot in the door of your mind and send demonic influences to you. Then, without you even being aware, some of his evil forces—demons take up residence in your soul. Everything about your life becomes tainted with falsehood, suspicion, fear, and imagined wrongs.

Even your body is affected. You develop headaches, blood pressure problems, sickness and disease. I'm not saying all this type of illness is caused from demonization, nor am I saying Christians can't have illness. I'm only saying that opening yourself up to the "wiles" of the devil increases your chances of experiencing these and many other maladies.

- Fantasy is vain imagination. Vain means empty, fruitless. It is the Hebrew word meaning to do/deal falsely, be false, trick, cheat.
- Fantasy is the birthing bed for jealousy and distrust.
  - Because we think it, then meditate on it, we begin to believe it has or will happen.
    - A neighbor I grew up with watched my relationship with my boyfriend. Decades later we bumped into each other and in his mind he and I had been a couple. In reality we had never even had an extended conversation. He carried bitterness because he perceived that I had dumped him. This was supposed to have happened on a particular date which was actually when my family moved to another state.

- Fantasy causes men and women to become derailed in their marriages, jobs, and destinies. Let me share a true story about a man I've known all his life.
  - At a very young age, two and half to three, he developed a vivid fantasy life. Among other things, he saw himself as a great bear hunter. He would kill bears all day then when the family came home no one was allowed to sit on the sofa or chairs because they were covered with his kills. The family actually sat in the floor until he went to bed or out to play.

    At age four or five he experienced his first "trick or treat" expedition. One house he went to with his brother and sister, to did not have candy to offer, rather they gave him an incantation. He had dressed up like Superman and took on that persona. He put his costume on ever day and went from house to house on his street asking for treats. When he got home from his outings he would take off the costume and enjoy his treats.

    As he grew older he continued taking on personas of comic book and movie characters. He became more and more ruthless and rebellious, even cruel. He is said to have harmed many people. Though today he is a pastor in a Christian church, he still struggles with violence, lies, and control. He has a very difficult time discerning right and wrong.

    He has always been able to see in the spirit realm and was called to a deliverance ministry. He has never stepped into the fullness of his destiny.

- Fantasy is an open door to satan and his minions.
  - They can ascertain what's going on in our bodies by the way we are react to the fantasy. When they "see" our train of thought by reading our physical reactions, they magnify the erotic and sensual, the anger and violence. They stir up our emotions and capture us with lies and vanity.

If you continue fantasizing, soon, bad habits form in other

areas of your life and all the while, you think you're just playing. Soon, without your knowing when or how it happened, nothing in your life is what it appears to be. You have become a victim of your own mind and a casualty of fantasy.

The only way out is through the Cross of Christ—acknowledging your helplessness and your need of intervention—crying out for forgiveness—crying out for relief and deliverance—repenting for choosing the wrong road:

> *"Jesus! Son of God! Please hear my cry! I need help! I need you! Please forgive me of all my sins. Renew my mind and deliver my soul. Create a clean heart and renew a right spirit within me. I renounce satan and all his works. I accept you as my Lord and my Savior. Please come into my heart, live in me and be Lord of my life."*

If you have prayed this prayer for the first time, you have just grabbed hold of the lifeline of Salvation through Jesus Christ, Son of the Living God. You have given Jesus permission to help you and save you. It would be a very good thing to contact a charismatic, full gospel, or Pentecostal—a Spirit-filled church in the area where you live. They will be able to help you, guiding you out of the labyrinth of darkness you have formed around yourself.

Now, any time your mind begins to wander into fantasy, do not permit yourself to do so. Simply say, "Jesus, help me. Show me Your way." Get a Bible and begin meditating on the Word of God. Begin training your senses to know the difference between right and wrong, truth and lies [Hebrews 5:14].

*　*　*

My song of love for you.

My heart of love for you.

You're as the stars of heaven shining brightly in the day.

You're as refreshing water from a mountain stream,

Even as refreshing as crisp mountain air.

Your heart-fire burns brightly,

Flamed by passion for the Holy.

The fire of your eyes project My love.

Your desire is My desire.

Your love has grown from Mine.

You are as gold refined

And

As silver seven times.

You are a precious jewel,

A pearl that is Mine.

(From visitation 2007 Velma Crow)

*　*　*

IMAGINATION:

Unlike fantasy which engages our soul, imagination engages our spirit so we can commune with God.

The further in time civilization moved from the Garden of Eden, the colder hearts became toward God. For thousands of years countless numbers of people imagined by the hearing of their ears that there is a true God who created everything we see. Job said it this way in Chapter 42, verse 5: *I had heard of You [only] by the hearing of the ear, but now my [spiritual] eye sees You.*

> *For that which is known about God is evident to them and made plain in their inner consciousness, because God [Himself] has shown it to them. For ever since the creation of the world His invisible nature and attributes, that is, His eternal power and divinity, have been made intelligible and clearly discernible in and through the things that have been made (His handiworks). So [men] are without excuse [altogether without any defense or justification].* Romans 1:19-22.

You can see by the above scripture, that it is possible, even without the Holy Scriptures—The Bible, to know by our spirit, see with our spiritual eyes and hear with our spiritual ears. These faculties develop as we become aware of and practiced in the communication system God established to communicate with all creation. He has bestowed this gift of communication upon us and established it within us. We refer to it as "imagination."

There are two Hebrew words in the Bible that are sometimes translated "imagination:"

- Strong's #3336, means: form, framing, purpose, framework, pottery, graven image, man (as formed from the dust), as well as imagination or devise (intellectual framework).

- Strong's #4906 means show-piece, a figure, image, idol, picture, conceit as well as imagination.

There are two Greek words in the Bible that are sometimes translated "imagination:"

- Strong's #1261 means thought, reasoning, doubtful, disputing as well as imagination.
- Strong's #1271 means mind, understanding, and imagination; the mind as a faculty of understanding; the mind, i.e. spirit way of thinking and feeling. It is a compound word formed from a combination of two other words Strong's #1223 and #3563.
  - o Strong's #1223 means by, through, with, for, and because of .
  - o Strong's #3563 means reason in the narrower sense as the capacity for spiritual truth, the higher powers of the soul, the faculty of perceiving divine things, of recognizing good and hating evil. The power of judging and considering soberly, calmly and impartially. This word is from the root word Strong's # 1097 meaning "to know."

For the Jew, knowing something goes beyond mere knowledge. In their understanding, one does not know something until the outworking of it is manifested in one's conduct.

Wow! Think of that! What would happen around us and in our lives if we purposed our mind, our spirit, to develop a greater capacity for spiritual truth, the higher powers of the soul, the perceiving of divine things and of recognizing good and hating evil? Can you imagine the implications of that? Can you picture what would happen if a community got together in such an effort, using their imaginations to increase their capacity for spiritual truth and development of the higher powers of their souls? What if people recognized and strived to recognize good and hate evil? Imagine the change in the atmosphere. Imagine the change in our relationships as our attitudes toward one another were flavored with recognizing good. How about if we confronted evil? Would it then have room to thrive in our community? In our nation? Is it possible that we could root out evil and develop goodness, kindness, and love?

By thinking this way we have activated our imagination. Our spirit is engaged and our communion open to God. Our soul/flesh is not engaged. We are not inciting our flesh with hatred, lust, greed, or any other negative enemy enticing, self serving attitude. Rather our minds, our hearts are set on things above Colossians 3:1-2.

When we begin purposefully seeking communication and communion with God—Father, Son and Holy Spirit— readily respond. They are eager for us to seek them and for us to hear and respond to them. For centuries they have been relegated to such a tiny portion of our consciousness that we—mankind—have become lukewarm and powerless. That is not God's plan for us. We are to walk in authority with dominion and power. We are to be His representatives on Earth, ambassadors of the God above all gods.

For some reason we seem to need permission of some earthly sort to even attempt to hear from heaven. Unfortunately, for many of us the thought of actually seeing a heavenly being is absolutely beyond belief. However, as we read the Bible we find numerous accounts where ordinary people not only saw and heard from that dimension, but also experienced visitations even of the Lord following His ascension. Some were lifted up. Others were transported from one location to another. There are people who actually do experience these things even today. The main difference between us and those people is our belief system. We need to have our senses practiced and our heart set to believe that through Christ the impossible is really possible and natural.

God is eager to commune with us as He did in the garden. (*As I'm typing this, I see the Lord stand up excitedly and hear Him encouraging me to continue boldly proclaiming these truths.*) He hears not only our verbal words but our thoughts. AND He responds to both our words and our thoughts. There is no difference to Him between the two.

Our earthly voice was given to speak things into this realm. Things such as:

- Authority
- Peace
- Love
- Corrections to the atmosphere
- Cancel things past
- Open the door for things in the future
- Defeat the enemy of our souls and of our Lord
- To take dominion
- To proclaim the acceptable day of the Lord
- Yes, to communicate with one another.

Indeed the counterfeit is out there. If you confuse fantasy with imagination you can get derailed. There are two keys to avoid this mix-up. One key is to not engage soulish tendencies and move into fantasy. Keep our mind/spirit centered on God. The master key is to know the Lord—know His voice—know His presence.

- We learn to recognize His voice through actually developing a relationship with the Word of God—The Bible.
  - He says, ***The sheep that are My own*** *hear and are listening to **My voice**; and **I know them**, and they follow Me* [John 10:27].

29

- The more we meditate on His Word, the more our thoughts align with His thoughts and our ways align with His ways.
- His Word begins to "live" in us and change us, spirit, soul and body.
  - Then, the more clearly we hear and understand His voice and the more quickly we respond to Him.
- We learn to know and recognize His presence through worship.
  o Great deliverance and healing come through praising and worshipping Him.
  o A hunger for His presence is developed during worship.

You see, it isn't enough to know about Him. Even memorizing scripture is not enough. We need to know Him on a personal basis. As we develop this personal relationship, everything about us begins being redeemed. Even the glory light that covered Adam and Eve begins to be reestablished. This happens through communion. Communion leads to relationship and takes place via our imaginations.

On Earth, we have GPS (Global Positioning System). When we are positioned correctly in the spirit, we have **GCS** (God's Communication System) which is our redeemed, sanctified Imagination.

When we come to know His voice He begins drawing us to Himself, into deeper relationship. We actually become friends with Him. Abraham was a friend of God [2 Chronicles 20:7]. John the Beloved was given access to know things to come—see the book of Revelation. Paul was taken into the third heaven, whether in the body or out of the body, he didn't know [2 Corinthians 12:2-3]. We'll discuss these things in more detail in a later chapter.

The main thing is, we need to have our *senses and mental*

faculties trained by practice to discern what is right ^{Hebrews 5:14}.

All the prophets used imagination to commune with God. They had no reference to be able to check out their experiences. Though many things were written down, there were no printing presses and no method of distribution to propagate such knowledge. There was no Bible with the accounts of what others had seen. These men and women became our stop-check—a way to assure us we are hearing and seeing by the Spirit of the Living God.

Communing with God is trusting Him with your inmost man—the very essence of your being. He is trustworthy and well able to lead us to Himself. He's not a man that He should lie or prove to be unfaithful. He is faithful and true. The love He has for us is beyond anything our earth language can explain or our human mind can comprehend.

As we develop relationship and trust we can be talking with Him "here" one moment and bowing before His throne the next. Perhaps we find ourselves walking with Him along the shore of the Sea of Galilee or sitting on the lip of heaven overlooking the universe, watching as God's Word continues performing what He sent it to do—creating, expanding in every direction, enlarging the universe as our scientist are proving every day. His Word never expires until it has performed everything He sent it to do.

As we begin practicing His presence and communing with Him, there will be times when fantasy tries to apprehend our mind. At other times the duties of the day draw us. We might start thinking about a grocery list. All of these can rob us of a special experience of communion with the Lord. But the more we keep our mind centered on Him the deeper our relationship grows.

At first it's a little like training a puppy. It takes constant attention until it's trained. Our mind goes off on a tangent—we pull it back. Don't allow it to get into . . .

- Worry, because it never resolves anything.
- Fear, because it only makes things look bigger than they are.
- Manipulation, because it always results in hurting someone.
- Soulish fantasies, because they only lead to sin.

If you give in to these and/or other distractions, you're robbing yourself. Often, distraction leads to giving the devil an open door to bring in some other form of dirt for us to deal with before we can get back into communion with the Lord.

You will guard him and keep him in perfect and constant peace whose mind [both its inclination and its character] is stayed on You, because he commits himself to You, leans on You, and hopes confidently in You ^{Isaiah 26:3}.

So trust in the Lord (commit yourself to Him, lean on Him, hope confidently in Him) forever; for the Lord God is an everlasting Rock [the Rock of Ages] ^{Isaiah 26:4}.

* * *

HEARING GOD:

When I first became aware of the Lord pursuing me for deeper relationship and drawing me toward visitation, He often spoke to me in voices of those I considered to be my mentors. Sometimes I heard Benny Hinn talking to me. The next time it might be Kenneth Copeland. One evening as I was on my end-of-day walk with my little dog, Joyce Meyer's face appeared before me and began teaching me. I knew it was the Lord so I said, "Lord, why do You always talk to me in someone else's voice.

"Because you don't listen to Me," was His reply.

I didn't know the sound of His voice. Often His voice sounds like our own—our thoughts. Sometimes it is the unmistakable voice of Many Waters. Other times it is like Rolling Thunder. His voice can be as soft as a turtle dove or as quick as a surgeon's scalpel. How we hear and how we see is totally dependent upon relationship.

When you begin entering into visitation with the Lord, if you have had extreme, life changing experiences—your first several visitations will most likely be brief and all about you. You will probably see yourself at the age of the first wounding—the first time you were not able to deal with a frightening or hurtful situation. I was six, one friend was three and another thirteen.

As you continue in visitation with the Lord you will see yourself mature as your soul is healed. You will gain a more clear understanding of your purpose and begin understanding the mysteries of God.

The time will come when He will take call on you at inconvenient times and in uncomfortable places to do exploits in the spirit realm. You may even move into physical transportations as Phillip the deacon and Elijah did. Accounts of such experiences are being shared today even in denominational circles where things such as this have rarely happened in the past.

Living by/under the principles of this world we cannot do what we have been designed and commissioned to do. We must step into our natural habitat—life in Christ often referred to as life in the Spirit . . . .

- Unafraid of the wind and waves of this world.
- Wrapped in the confidence of His love.
- Doing what we see the Father do.
- Saying what we hear Him say.

Dare to be a world changer. Dare to desire and believe you, too, can enter into that naturally supernatural relationship with the Living God.

* * * * * * * *

EXERCISES

1. Enter into worship with your heart and mind set on Jesus.
    a. Following worship, write your perceptions.
2. Meditate on the experiences of others in the Word of God.
3. Allow yourself to desire a face-to-face relationship with the Living God.
    a. Give yourself permission to believe it can actually happen to/for you.
4. Even if you have only a few minutes to focus on Him, He will manifest Himself to you.
    a. Give Him every opportunity.

SEEK FIRST THE KINGDOM

Worship should be primary,
Teaching second.

Patricia King – "A Gospel of Power"

But seek, (aim at and strive after) first of all His kingdom and His righteousness, (His way of doing and being right) then all these taken together will be given you besides. Matthew 6:33 .

If there was a book on how to become a human being, the above scripture should be the first sentence. Of equal importance is:

Jesus answered, If a person [really loves] Me, he will keep My Word, [obey My teaching]; and My Father will love him, and We will come to him and make Our home (abode, special dwelling place) with him. John 14:23 .

Both before the Cross of Christ and after, the Word of God is full of examples of . . .

- actual visitations
- transportations
- times when people heard the voice of God and angels
- times when people were lifted up into the heavens and saw and heard marvelous, even unspeakable things in the Spirit.

Familiarize yourself with these encounters so you will not be drawn into error. Although our encounters may differ somewhat from the scriptural examples, if only because we live in an age of television, computers, cell phones and space travel, the more familiar you are with the scriptural accounts the more readily you will perceive the Spirit of Truth versus the spirit of deception.

But solid food is for full-grown men, for those whose senses and mental faculties are trained <u>by practice</u> to discriminate and distinguish between what is morally good and noble and what is evil and contrary either to divine or human law ^{Hebrews 5:14}.

I have still many things to say to you, but you are not able to bear them or to take them upon you or to grasp them now.

But when He, the Spirit of Truth, the Truth-giving Spirit comes, He will guide you into all the truth—(the whole, full truth).

For He will not speak His own message[on His own authority]; but He will tell whatever He hears [from the Father; He will give the message that has been given to Him], and He will announce and declare to you the things that are to come [that will] happen in the future.

He will honor and glorify Me, because He will take of,

(receive and draw upon) what is Mine and will reveal, declare, disclose, transmit it to you. Everything that the Father has is Mine. That is what I meant when I said that He, the Spirit, will take the things that are Mine and will reveal, (declare, disclose, and transmit) it to you John 16:12-15.

Allow the Spirit of Truth to guide you into a deeper, more personal—even intimate relationship with our Lord and Father.

In our study we'll start out in Genesis with Adam and Eve. After God made "the man" and put him in the garden He began talking to him.

And the Lord God commanded the man saying, You may freely eat of every tree of the garden; but of the tree of the knowledge of good and evil and blessing and calamity you shall not eat, for in the day that you eat of it you shall surely die? Genesis 2:16-17.

As long as Adam and Eve lived in the Garden, they not only heard the voice of the Lord God, they also enjoyed His manifest presence. After the fall, they were no longer covered in His glory; they were mere flesh—naked, afraid and ashamed. BUT! They still heard the sound of the Lord God walking in the Garden. They still heard Him talking and were able to respond to Him; however, knowing they were different, they hid themselves.

And they heard LORD God walking in the garden in the cool of the day: but Adam and his wife hid themselves from the presence of the LORD God among the trees of the garden.

And the LORD God called to Adam, and said to him, Where are you?

He said, I heard the sound of You [walking] in the garden, and I was afraid because I was naked; and I hid myself.

And He said, Who told you that you were naked? Have you eaten of the tree of which I commanded you that you should not eat? Genesis 3:8-11 *.*

You see? Adam and Eve had sinned through disobedience and rebellion. It wasn't a thought out thing, it was something many of us do regularly. We' may vow to not do or to do a particular thing and then catch ourselves in the middle of it and wonder how we got there. They may have thought and wanted to say, "We didn't mean to. It just happened!" They did make excuses, but that didn't matter. They had sinned and their action couldn't be erased and is still affecting the earth and everything on it to this day. They needed redemption and none had been made. Yet, they still heard and understood God. He still had conversations with them.

Generations later when their children were grown, they and their children and their children's children were still able to hear, understand and respond to the voice of God. For example, Let's look at Cain: though he did not <u>walk</u> with God, he did <u>talk </u>with Him even as his father and mother did.

As a matter of fact, a couple of conversations between the Lord and Cain are recorded in Genesis 4. The Lord actually warned Cain about his attitude. Verses 6 and 7 have a good lesson for us:

And the Lord said to Cain, Why are you angry? And why do you look sad and depressed and dejected? If you do well, will you not be accepted? And if you do not do well, sin crouches at your door; its desire is for you, but you must master it.

- Sin waits for us, watches at the door of our heart. Don't give the devil an attitude to work with. We really need to keep our hearts, our minds, stayed, centered, God.
  - That means we should follow hard after righteousness and don't let comparisons (jealousy, contention or strife) gain a foothold in our soul.

The Lord knew what was in Cain's heart; he was corrupted with jealousy which bloomed into the act of murder. Yet, he still, clearly, heard the voice of God and bargained with Him concerning his punishment.

God has never stopped talking to us. We, mankind, have become dull of hearing. We don't expect to hear and normally don't. But that can and should change.

There are several experiences related in the Bible where someone we might think could never hear God, heard the voice of God—even conversed with Him. For instance, Abram, whose father made idols [Genesis 12]. Upon hearing God's instruction, Abram left his homeland and went into a land he didn't know and where he had no family or friends. God continued to lead Abram, talking with him, encouraging him, saving him to become the root of the nation of Israel. God changed Abram's name and called him His friend [2 Chronicles 20:7; James 2:23].

Abram's new name was Abraham. I've heard it said that the "ha" in AbraHAm represents the sound of breath—the Spirit of God. Actually, God changed Abram's name to one that would declare and proclaim his destiny. God put his "super" on Abram's "natural" so he went from being known as Abram, "exalted father," to being proclaimed Abraham, "father of a multitude." Every time anyone spoke the new name, "Abraham," they were declaring, yes—prophesying, "You are the father of a multitude." His name change renewed his body as well as establishing his future.

Another one we might not expect to hear from God was Sarah's handmaiden, Hagar. Hagar was an Egyptian. Yet, following a conversation with the angel of the Lord, she swallowed her pride and returned to the tent of her mistress. Now, in this instance the word translated 'angel' is from an unused root meaning, to dispatch as a deputy. So, Hagar had a conversation with a "deputy" from heaven who told her not only that her child would be a son, but also what she was to name him and who/what he would become ^{Genesis 16:7-12}. Later when it was the Lord's time for her to leave Abram, God heard the voice of her son, Ishmael. God spoke to her and opened her eyes to see a well of water, thereby saving her own life as well as that of her son. And God made of him a great nation as He had promised ^{Genesis 21:17-18}.

There are many other instances too numerous to mention in which men and women, even children heard the voice of God or an angel. We'll discuss a few here:

- Abimelech, in Genesis 20, conversed with God, bargaining for his very life.
- When Samuel was very young, in 1 Samuel 3, God called his name three times in the night but Samuel did not know it was the Lord. Knowing someone was calling him, he responded to Eli. The third time Eli told him to say, "Speak, Lord, for your servant is listening," When Samuel responded to the Lord, he received a harsh word to deliver to Eli the High Priest.
  - o Many of us can relate to Samuel here. I can't tell you how many times I've said, "Was that really You, Lord?"

**When you hear your name being called or
You perceive a presence, and you don't really know**

who or what it is,
respond even if just to say,
"Who are you?"
Or,
"Do you have a message for me?"

- Enoch is so inspiring to me. Enoch *walked in habitual fellowship with God; and he was not, for God took him home with Him* ^{Genesis 5:24}. *He did not glimpse death and was not found because God had translated him* ^{Hebrews 11:5}.

That's really what God wants for us. He wants to take us home with Him. I would love to read Enoch's book. I've seen the volumes of Enoch but have not read them as of this writing.

By the way, I'm sure you know, we are being written about in heaven. There are more books than we know there. Malachi tells of a book of remembrance.

Then those who feared the Lord talked often one to another; and the Lord listened and heard it, and a book of remembrance was written before Him of those who reverenced and worshipfully feared the Lord and who thought on His name ^{Malachi 3:16}.

All of this and much more was before the Cross of Christ!

We won't take time to go over all the experiences Moses had with God. He appeared to him and spoke to him at various times and in various ways. And, *God talked to Moses face to face as friend talks to friend* ^{Exodus 33:11}.

God is so awesome. He wanted all the Children of Israel to commune with Him and gave them all the opportunity. But they were afraid. They prepared to meet God. He told Moses to sanctify the people, have them to wash their clothes and be ready by the third day. (Does that remind you of anything?)

They did everything in preparation for the big day. But when they got to the mountain and saw the cloud, the smoke, the lightening and heard the thunder they became afraid. They trembled with fear and fell back and stood afar off and told Moses, *You speak to God then tell us what He says* Exodus 20:18-21. Then Moses drew near to the thick darkness and the Lord said, *Tell the people, you have seen for yourselves that I have talked with you from heaven* Exodus 19:9—20:22.

Later, the Lord told Moses to bring Aaron, Nadab, Abihu and seventy of the elders of Israel to the mountain. So this group went to the mountain:

> *And they saw the God of Israel, that is, a convincing manifestation of His presence, and under His feet it was like pavement of bright sapphire stone, like the very heavens in clearness. And upon the nobles of the Israelites He laid not His hand to conceal himself from them, to rebuke their daring, or to harm them but they saw the manifestation of the presence of God, and ate and drank* Exodus 24:9-11.

In other words, they saw God and lived to tell about it!

While we're in the wilderness, let's look at one more thing, Deuteronomy 23:14:

> *For the LORD thy God walks in the midst of your camp, to deliver you, and to give up your enemies before you; therefore shall your camp be holy: that He may see nothing indecent among you, and turn away from you.*

Now how real is that!? The Lord God, before the cross, walked in the midst of the camp!

What's He going to see when He walks through our house? Is there anything that would make Him turn away or will He feel at ease? Just suppose He's going to visit some evening, a surprise visit, and He walks through your (or my) "camp" and sees what's on TV or hears what we're talking about. Would He turn away?

* * * * * * * * *

Of course, we're all familiar with Samuel, Elijah, Elisha, Deborah, Daniel and Ezekiel, as well as Job, Hosea, Amos, etc. They heard God. They didn't have the written Word. THEIR LIVES BECAME THE WRITTEN WORD. They had to get fresh manna—direction—straight from the Lord God or angels. It wasn't uncommon to have angelic encounters in that day or encounters with the Lord.

I do want to share something I learned about Deborah. I found this in the supporting notes in the Amplified Bible, bottom of page 289.

- "According to Numbers 11:25, the prophetic gift has its source in the "Spirit of the Lord." The prophet is a spokesman of God and for God." As for Deborah it is said, "The objective Spirit of her God elevates her above her people, above heroes before and after her. Not only the ecstasy of enthusiasm, but also the calm wisdom of that Spirit Who informs the law dwells in her."
  o That's about RELATIONSHIP! Yes, she was a chosen vessel, but her willingness to have a living connection with the living God made the difference in her life.

Let's take a good look at Gideon, Judges 6:11-8:25. The crux of his story is that the Lord evidently presented Himself to Gideon in various forms.

- When He first appeared to Gideon in Chapter 6, verses 11 and 14, He presented Himself as the *Angel of the Lord*. This is also the form in which He presented Himself throughout most of the Gideon saga.
  - o Now, the word angel is defined in Strong's (#4397) as a deputy, messenger, representative but also as the theophanic angel. Theophanic means an appearance of God.
  - o The word "Lord" there is Jehovah – the Existing One.
- In verse 20, *the angel of God*.
  - o Here, the word angel is the same as above.
  - o God here is "Elohiym." It's a plural word, indicating multiple rulers, Father, Son, Holy Spirit; some even say the holy angels are included as well. I'm told the Jews consider this to be the heavenly court or council.
    - ▪ So, a deputy from the heavenly court was dispatched to speak with Gideon.
- In verse 34 the *Spirit of the Lord* came upon Gideon.
  - o After this, most of the time when Gideon is speaking to God—he is speaking to Elohiym.

So in just a few verses we see that Father, Son and Holy Spirit as well as angels interacted with Gideon. But there is a catch and a great lesson for us at the end of Chapter 8, verse 27. Gideon had made an ephod to honor God but it became a snare to him and to his house, his entire family, as well as his servants because he established it as an object of worship. This is where the "God thing" Gideon was doing under God's direction changed to a good thing Gideon decided to do. Good things are never good enough if they are not under the direction of God. They can become a snare that prevents us from continuing to walk in God's plan for us.

Consider the book of Job:

I had heard of You only by the hearing of the ear, but now my [spiritual] eye sees You ^{Job 42:5}.

It wasn't only Job who heard the Lord. Eliphaz also heard and it wasn't a comforting word the Lord spoke to him.

After the Lord had spoken the previous words to Job, the Lord said to Eliphaz the Temanite, My wrath is kindled against you and against your two friends, for you have not spoken of Me the thing that is right, as My servant Job has. Now, therefore take seven bullocks and seven rams and go to My servant Job and offer up for yourselves a burnt offering; and My servant Job shall pray for you, for I will accept his prayer that I deal not with you after your folly, in that you have not spoken of Me the thing that is right, as My servant Job has ^{Job 42:7-8}.

Oh my! Correction—instruction—warning—mercy and grace!

* * * * * * * * *

Now, we won't be able to touch on every experience reported in the Bible, but there are some reports here which open doors of possibilities for us. As an example, let's take a quick look at Psalm 32. David is pouring himself out to the Lord as was his custom. We'll start in verse 7:

You are a hiding place for me; You, Lord preserve me from trouble. You surround me with songs and shouts of deliverance. **Selah** *(pause, and calmly think of that)* ^{Psalms 32:7}.

Now while David is pausing to think about that, the Lord begins talking to him and while he's thinking, the Lord speaks to him:

I, the Lord, will instruct you and teach you in the way you should go: I will counsel you with My eye upon you ^{Psalm} _{32:8}.

As you study the Psalms you'll find a number of such instances. Here's a key we don't want to miss:

┅ When we're studying, praying or meditating, we should take time to pause and think.

It just may be that while we're pausing,

the Lord will speak to us!

We can read of Daniel, who was visited by the angel Gabriel who stands by the throne of God ^{Daniel 8:16}. He had numerous encounters with angels.

Daniel's three close friends, Shadrach, Meshach, and Abednego were cast into a fire so hot it burned up the people who cast them into the flames. They were joined by *"a fourth Man like the Son of God"* ^{Daniel 3:24}! Not only did they not burn but their clothes did not even carry the smell of smoke when they were called forth from the furnace ^{Daniel 3:27}. The pagan king saw with his natural eyes. When he looked into the furnace, he saw not only the three walking around in the fire unbound and unharmed, he also saw the fourth Man ^{Daniel 3:23-28}.

┅ The Lord is willing to be seen. We need to be willing to see.

Ezekiel had numerous experiences with heavenly creatures and even was held by the hair of his head between heaven and earth ^{Ezekiel 8:3}.

Let's skip on over to Zechariah. This is a wonderful book. I know there are some pretty severe things in here but I'm speaking in regard to RELATIONSHIP. Chapter 3 is one of the doors of possibility the Lord opened for me one day as I was praying during my lunch hour at work.

Then the guiding angel showed me Joshua the high priest standing before the Angel of the Lord, and Satan standing at Joshua's right hand to be his adversary and to accuse him. And the Lord said to Satan, The Lord rebuke you, O Satan! Even the Lord Who now and habitually chooses Jerusalem, rebuke you! Is not this returned captive Joshua a brand plucked out of the fire?

Now Joshua was clothed with filthy garments and was standing before the Angel of the Lord. And He spoke to those who stood before Him, saying; Take away the filthy garments from him. And He said to Joshua, Behold, I have caused your iniquity to pass from you and I will clothe you with rich apparel.

And I, Zechariah, said, Let them put a clean turban on his head. So they put a clean turban on his head and clothed him with [rich] garments. And the Angel of the Lord stood by ^{Zechariah 3:1-5}.

IS THAT EXCITING OR WHAT?!

⊷Zechariah spoke into a vision and the angels obeyed him just as they did the Angel of the Lord!

Bless, affectionately, gratefully praise the Lord, you His angels, you mighty ones who do His commandments, ***hearkening to the voice of His word*** ^{Psalms 103:20}.

We are the voice of His word on earth when we speak what He puts in our mouth! Hearkening is the Hebrew verb that means, "to hear, listen to, obey." When this was made clear to me, I was praying for my pastor who had purchased a short wave radio station but the transmitter had been struck by lightning. This was a major acquisition for the body of Christ because it is the only privately owned short wave station with a global footprint. I was praying for the resources, equipment, manpower, etc., to repair the transmitter and get the station back on the air. As I prayed I saw my pastor in a vision, standing before me. I expected to see more but when I didn't I said, "What, Lord. What are you trying to show me?"

The Lord said, "Read Zechariah, chapter 3."

I read it and said, "What?"

The Lord said, "Read it again."

Three times I read that chapter before I got it. **I was to speak into the vision and command the angels to bring Pastor Mawire what he needed to get this station on the air.**

I have spoken to angels directly and knew we are to co-labor with them. I knew they are sent to assist those who are heirs of salvation—still—I had never considered the possibility of speaking into a vision! I had had visions for years but had not purposely participated in them. I don't know how much of a part my participation in that vision played in the overall plan, but the materials and finances did come in. The station that had been established to send New Orleans jazz around the world now broadcasts the Gospel of Jesus Christ 24/7. Praise God! Hallelujah!

We could go on and on through the Old Testament. It's chock full of what we consider to be supernatural experiences, such as Daniel, Ezekiel, Joshua . . .

- Elisha: Even his dry bones retained the glory of God so that when the body of a dead man was thrown in upon them the man was raised to life again [2 Kings 13:21].

- Isaiah: He saw the Lord on His throne and the seraphim flying around crying, "Holy." Isaiah felt unworthy not only because of his own sin, but the sin of his people. One of the seraphim got a coal from the altar, flew down and touched Isaiah's mouth saying, "Your iniquity and guilt are taken away, and your sin is completely atoned for and forgiven." Then the seraphim gave Isaiah a message to tell the people [Isaiah 6:1-9].

- Joshua: The Children of Israel needed more time during a battle, so Joshua spoke to the Lord and the sun and the moon stood still for about a day until the Israelites defeated their enemies. God obeyed the voice of a man [Joshua 10:12-14].

- God even caused the shadow of a sundial to backup ten degrees (steps) as a sign to Abimelech that He was going to heal him and add 15 years to his life [2 Kings 20:1-11].

There are so many other examples of experiences well worth the effort and time to ferret out. I encourage you to read through the Bible specifically to encounter the people who do exploits for their God. Read their experiences and know that God is not a respecter of persons [Acts 10:24]. He'll use anyone who is willing to be used, and sometimes, even those who resist.

NOW, LET'S COME TO THIS SIDE OF THE CROSS IN SCRIPTURE.

- The first visitation mentioned in the New Testament was that of the Angel of the Lord visiting Zachariah, the High Priest, while he performed his duties in the temple. Because He did not believe what the Angel of the Lord said was possible, he became mute until the promised child was born ^{Luke 1:5-25}.

➻ Our unbelief may not delay or negate the promise, however, there may be consequences.

- The second recorded visitation we encounter in the New Testament is Mary and the angel, Gabriel. After Gabriel delivered the message AND Mary accepted the assignment, Holy Spirit overshadowed her and implanted life in her womb just as when He moved, hovered, over the waters in Genesis ^{Luke 1:26-38}.
  - o Mary immediately accepted the Word though it could carry dire circumstances. She could be killed. But she trusted God to protect her and bring the promise about. As soon as she said, "Yes," Holy Spirit overshadowed her—hovered over her to bring forth life.
    - ▪ I'm working on making that level of surrender my lifestyle. Too often I find myself informing God of things that I feel certain, were He aware of, He probably wouldn't ask such a thing. After all He only knows the beginning, the end, and everything in the middle! (Hope you see my humor. If you don't I'm sure you see my dilemma—SELF!)
- The birth and early years of Jesus are surrounded by numerous visitations to various people:
  - o Shepherds heard and saw angels making proclamations and singing ^{Luke 2:8-15}.

- o Wise men or kings from the East, after being directed to Jerusalem by a star, were warned by God in a dream to not tell King Herod where to find Jesus. They left Bethlehem by a different route to avoid another contact with Herod [Matthew 2:12].

- Joseph, Mary's husband, had numerous visitations by dreams or visions in the night.
  - o He was told to take Mary as his wife because, the Child within her was conceived of the Holy Ghost [Matthew 1:18, 20].
  - o He moved his small family a number of times, carefully guarding them, always under the direction of angelic communication [Matthew 2:13, Matthew 2:19-21].

- Here's a visitation not many of us would want to experience though we know it happens even today:
  - o When Jesus went to the wilderness, satan, himself, showed up and tempted Jesus in every way possible.
    - ▪ Jesus kept His mind stayed, centered on righteousness. He made sure there was nothing within Himself that was in common with satan.
      - Now, satan took Him various places, tempting Him with all sorts of promises.
  - o After Jesus triumphed over every offer satan made, angels came and strengthened Him. He had been fasting forty days in a harsh terrain with no shelter. [Matthew 4:1-11].

- In the Garden of Gethsemane, an angel strengthened Jesus while His disciples slept [Luke 22:43].

- Following Jesus' resurrection:
  - o Mary Magdalene along with Mary, the mother of James, and Salome, went to the tomb and saw a young man (many transcripts interpret this to be an angel) who told them that Jesus had risen. He also told them to go

tell the disciples that He had risen and would meet them in Galilee $^{\text{Mark 16:1-8}}$.

o John and Peter went back to the tomb with Mary Magdalene but saw nothing. They left but Mary stayed, weeping and longing for the Lord. She stooped and looked into the tomb again and this time there were two angels sitting in there. They spoke to her and she responded to them. Turning away toward the garden she saw a man and when He spoke her name, she knew it was Jesus $^{\text{John 20, Mark 16}}$.

o Two disciples were going home from Jerusalem to Emmaus. Someone met them and walked along with them for a while. They had been talking about the events that had just happened in Jerusalem, the crucifixion and events following. This stranger expounded on scriptures with them. When they arrived at their house, they invited their fellow traveler to join them for dinner. When He broke the bread, they recognized Jesus. Then—He disappeared. The men hurried back to Jerusalem and told the other disciples everything that had happened but no one believed them $^{\text{Luke 24:13-33}}$.

o Jesus had already visited Peter $^{\text{Luke 24:34}}$.

o The eleven apostles and several of the disciples including those from Emmaus, were gathered behind closed doors talking about the reports of those who had seen Jesus, He appeared in their midst. Some of them were very frightened and thought He was a spirit. To prove to them He was real, Jesus told them to "handle" Him, touch His flesh and put their fingers in His wounds. Then He asked for some food. He ate and disappeared $^{\text{John 20:19-25}}$. Then eight days later, He appeared again $^{\text{John 20:26-31}}$.

- o He was seen again on the shores of the Sea of Galilee where He asked the disciples for some fish. This was the third time He was seen of them following His resurrection ^{John 21:1-14}.
- o He was seen by 500 ^{1 Corinthians 15:6}.
- o He was seen ascending into heaven ^{Acts 1:9-11}.
  - ▪ Angels were in attendance as well.
- Cornelius is very interesting. Though he was a devout man he was not a Jew. He was a Roman, a centurion, who venerated God and prayed continually. During prayer one day, an angel appeared in a vision and spoke to him giving him instructions to send men to Joppa and ask a man named Peter to come to Caesarea. He told Cornelius who Peter was staying with and where the house was located. Now, when Cornelius saw the angel he was frightened. However, he spoke and asked, *"What is it, Lord?"* ^{Acts 10:1-9}.
  - o There are two lessons in this short section of scripture.

☞ When we see an angel we should ask what he's there for.

☞ If the angel gives instructions, do what he says.

- The next day while Cornelius' men were still on their way to Joppa, Peter was on a roof top in a trance. The Lord was showing him the new order for the church—the expansion of the Body of Christ. When the trance ended, Holy Spirit said to Peter, *"There are three men looking for you. Go with them without hesitation for I have sent them."* Peter went and preached. Holy Spirit fell on the Romans and they spoke in tongues. So, Peter knew that this reformation was for all nations ^{Acts 10:9-48}.

- o As a Jewish man, Peter's experience would be like some of us going into a witches' coven or walking into a "house of ill repute." When we, under instruction of Holy Spirit, speak to even just one person, we have no idea how that will affect the Kingdom, nor how far reaching our obedience will be.
- Peter was in jail—asleep—when an angel "smote" him on the side to wake him, then led him out of the prison. When they came to an iron gate, the gate opened by itself. He went to a friend's house where they were having a prayer meeting (praying for Peter's release). When a servant girl went to see who was at the gate and saw it was Peter, she went back into the house and told the others. They said to her, "No, it's just his angel or messenger." But, Peter kept knocking. When the people went out to see who was there, they saw it was indeed Peter ^{Acts 12:5-17}.
  - o Interestingly, they were more able to believe that Peter's spirit or an angelic messenger was at the gate than that their prayers had been answered and Peter had escaped from prison.
- Philip, the deacon, was physically translated from one place to another on Earth! He was in the middle of a huge revival in which entire cities were transformed, accepting Jesus as Lord and Savior. The Lord sent him to the desert to speak to <u>one</u> man who just happened to be in a position to touch a nation. Then he, Philip, was picked up by the Spirit of God and deposited in a town about 34 miles away and the new convert did not see him again ^{Acts 8:39-40}!
  - o Oh! I'm eagerly anticipating that! Others today report having experienced it. I am convinced I will also and may have—whether in the body or out—I know not!
- Saul of Tarsus, an unbeliever and persecutor of the church, had an encounter with a bright light and heard the voice of

the Lord. Those with him heard a voice like thunder but didn't see anyone. The Lord and Saul conversed, and Saul was given instructions ^{Acts 9:1-9}.

○ God can speak to anyone at any time. He can turn hatred into devotion. He can transform our mission into His assignment for us and turn our destructive passions into zeal for the House of the Lord.

- This brings us to another man visited by the Lord, Ananias. The Lord gave Ananias instructions concerning Saul and Ananias argued with Him. He reminded the Lord that this Saul of Tarsus was one who was willing to do anything to stop the growth of the Church. He was a dangerous man. Despite his objections, Ananias did obey the Lord ^{Acts 9:12-18}.

○ How wonderful is that!? Even if we think the Lord may not have all the information on the situation, we need to trust Him and do what He says. I'm sure none of you have ever argued with the Lord but unfortunately that experience is part of my history.

- At one point Paul talks about "a man" being "caught up" into the third heaven and into Paradise, seeing things and hearing utterings that could not even be put into words. He didn't know if he was in the spirit or in the flesh—having a natural experience or a spiritual one ^{2 Corinthians 12:1-10}.

○ Caught up means, to seize, carry off by force, to seize on, claim for one's self eagerly, to snatch out or away.

▪ This phrase leads me to believe this was a physical translation (to be seized, carried off by force or snatched away). What an exciting possibility!

○ Heaven: Strong's lists several "possible definitions" including "the region above the sidereal heavens, <u>the seat of order of things eternal and consummately perfect where God dwells</u> and other heavenly beings."

- Paradise: This word is of oriental origin and possible definitions include garden, grand enclosure, hunting or pleasure ground, park, etc., even a part of Hades where souls of departed pious awaited resurrection. Also, the upper regions of the heavens.

⊷ Don't make logical excuses when the illogical happens. The Lord, Himself, does visit us from time to time. Dare to believe!

This is God's desire for all of us. He has claimed each of us for Himself by the shedding of His own blood. He has completely torn away the dividing veil that kept mankind from God and invites us to all come boldly into His presence [Matthew 27:51, Mark 15:38, Luke 23:45].

- The LORD, Himself, stood beside Paul and told him He was sending him to Rome [Acts 23:11].
- He spoke to Paul in the night by a vision [Acts 18:9].
  - We should pay attention to our dreams for the Lord, Himself, does speak in dreams and visions.
- John the Beloved, the Revelator, was "rapt in a vision" when a voice with the sound of a trumpet spoke to him. The voice invited him to, "Come up here," into the heavens to receive greater revelation. We read how the Lord, God and angels, spoke with him. During this encounter, John was taken twice by an angel to see the future and gain even deeper revelation and knowledge of things to come [Revelation 1, 17:3, 21:10].
  - I encourage you to re-read Revelation. It is an awesome book and carries a blessing to all who read it aloud in the assemblies!
- Perhaps, one of the most interesting of all visitations was on the Mount of Transfiguration [Matthew 17:1-6, Mark 9:1-8S].

In this account we see three ordinary men with Jesus in their current time in eternity. He was transfigured, saturated with the Glory of God, and they could see it! He was joined by Elijah, who, hundreds of years earlier had been taken up physically in a chariot without tasting death. Then! They are joined by another man, Moses, who, though he did die centuries earlier, there he was standing, talking with Jesus and Elijah in a physical body, conversing with them.

To make the experience "fully complete," God spoke out of heaven and the "earthly" men heard and understood. Sounds like, past, present and future coming together in one place, in one point of time.

OH! That stirs my spirit! A taste of eternity demonstrated on Earth for human eyes to see! How much are we missing of what God is doing around us today?!

Father! Open my eyes so I can see; my ears so I can hear. Increase my understanding. Purge my soul so I can perceive the things of the Spirit.

We could study endlessly about such experiences but I want to get on to practical application.

⮞ Jesus is our primary example.

He showed us by His daily life how to live and operate in the Kingdom of God. As the Son of Man, He . . .

- Demonstrated to us how to integrate the Kingdom of Heaven with this earthly realm.
- He exercised dominion through His authority as Son of Man, establishing Kingdom Rule on earth as it is in heaven.
- He took dominion over the elements as well as over demonic forces.

- Then—just so we didn't miss it, He sent a book we call the Holy Bible, to let us know of men and women who demonstrated these abilities, both before and after the cross.

This is a time when we will choose to purposely walk in dominion on earth and simultaneously access heavenly realms for the benefit of the Kingdom, or, we will choose to stay bound by the principles of this world and never know the full richness of relationship in Christ.

* * * * * * * * *

EXERCISES

1. Pray in the Spirit an additional five minutes every day.
   - Ask for interpretation.
     - o If you do not yet have your prayer language, ask Holy Spirit to give it to you. Ask Him for spiritual tongues.
2. Read the Word of God an additional five minutes every day.
   - Choose a "scripture of the day" to meditate on for enlightenment and strength.
3. Compile and keep an alphabetic list of words that describe your knowledge of and relationship with:
   - The Lord Jesus Christ:
     - o Example: Alpha, Bridegroom, Faithful One, Lover of My Soul, Savior, Ultimate Example, Wisdom, Xavier, etc.
   - Father God:
     - o Example: Omniscient, Omnipotent, Omnipresent, Provider, Source, Ultimate Authority, etc.
   - Holy Spirit:
     - o Example: Comforter, Constant Companion, Guide, Nurturer, Revealer, Stop-Check, Teacher, etc.
   - The Word of God:

- o Example: Absolute, Blueprint for Life, Truth, Xerox of the ages, etc.

(These lists will reveal to you the depth of your relationship and what areas need to be worked on or yielded to. Keep them updated as your relationship with the Father, Son, Holy Spirit and the Word deepens. These lists can be a source of strength and comfort.)

- As you meditate on these lists, search your heart for other names by which you want/need to know the Triune God.
- Ask Holy Spirit to enable you to "see" the aspects and attributes of God in your life and the lives of those around you.

*   *   *

4 May 2012, I was watching television while I ate my lunch. Suddenly, instead of James Garner in "The Rockford Files", I saw a very large, blue angel standing in front of the T.V. Blue light emanated from his clothes and skin. I asked him to speak—deliver the message.

"Go. Follow Him," said the angel, then, he began singing: *He will lead you where you want to go.*

(I thought, "I don't want to go where I want to go. I want to go where He wants me to be.) The angel became silent while I entertained my own thoughts. When I noticed that I quieted my thoughts.

The angel sang again.

I'm going to send you out two-by-two.
Where shall I send you?
You can run but you cannot hide.
I've got a plan and it will abide.
Between the Cherubim enter in.
The Secret Place is where to begin.
Follow Me now and enter in.
Follow Me now—let us begin.
Where I Am taking you, many others desire to go.
It's a chosen place for the chosen only,
Replete with revelation and anointing.
There the glory dwells and will abide on you.
It's the origin of the Well of My Presence.
You've got something. Don't let it go.
Dwell in My Life. Carry My Light.
Forbid not what you see nor what you hear.
The filling of My plan is drawing near.
I will fulfill. Hear Me calling. Hear.

*   *   *

UNCONDITIONAL LOVE

He's not withholding Himself from us,
We tend to withhold ourselves from Him.

The love of God is completely unconditional. He didn't die on the cross for those who could purge their own sins. He died for those of us who cannot. So, that includes EVERYONE!

It is very important to not allow feelings of guilt, shame, lack of confidence, or unworthiness keep you from allowing Him to visit with you face to face. The woman caught in the "very act of adultery" was instantly acceptable to Jesus. "Neither do I condemn you," were His words to her [John 8:11]. Neither does He condemn you or me. Look at 1 John 3:19-21, as a demonstration of how unconditional His great love is:

> *By this we shall come to know (perceive, recognize, and understand) that we are of the Truth, and can reassure (quiet, conciliate, and pacify) our hearts <u>in His presence</u>, whenever our hearts in [tormenting] self-accusation make us feel guilty and condemn us. [For we are in God's hands.] <u>For He is above and greater than our consciences (our hearts)</u>, and He knows (perceives and understands) everything [<u>nothing is hidden from Him</u>].*

Do you see? Even if we think ourselves unforgivable, He who looks on our heart and knows everything about us, is greater than our own heart, and He forgives us. Confess any known sin. David even prayed in Psalm 19:13, *"Keep back Your servant also from presumptuous sins; let them not have dominion over me! Then shall I be blameless and I shall be innocent and clear of great transgression."* Repent, turn away from error/sin and take a step in faith toward righteousness with the confidence that you are forgiven and free from even the stain of sin. For the Faithful One has said this through His servant, John the Beloved:

> *If we [freely] admit that we have sinned and confess our sins, He is faithful and just (true to His own nature and promises) and will forgive our sins [dismiss our lawlessness] and [continuously] cleanse us from all unrighteousness [everything not in conformity to His will in purpose, thought and action]* [1 John 1:9].

Then, come boldly into His presence—even to the Throne of Grace.

➻ Visitation is a time and place where truth is clearly revealed in such a loving way
that we are able to accept it and that truth we accept can have its delivering and healing effect on our souls.

When Zacchaeus wanted to see the Lord and climbed a tree because he was short, Jesus didn't say, "Who do you think you are?" No! He said, "Come on down and hurry up about it. I'm going to your house for dinner." (Luke 19, paraphrased) Even though this man had a reputation of being a sinner, Jesus wanted to spend time with him.

Now, Jesus didn't just want to have a little dinner. He said He would "abide" there. That word translated as "abide" means multiple things. In this instance:

- In reference to a place; to sojourn, tarry; not to depart; to continue to be present; to be held, kept, continually.

So, Jesus didn't just want to spend a few hours with Zacchaeus. He wanted to stay with Him. He wanted to make such a change in Zacchaeus that they would never part [Luke 19]. This is His plan for us too.

How about the woman at the well? Even before she was converted, Jesus said, *"If you knew Who this is that is saying to you, Give Me a drink, you would have asked Him [instead] and He would have given you living water* [John 4:10]. In that day Jewish men did not speak to/with Samaritans, let alone "women."

➻ You see? He's not withholding Himself from us. We are withholding ourselves from Him.

He is willing to break customs and traditions just for the possibility of a conversation with you. He knows the great effect you can and will have on people in your area of influence. Your testimony of His voice in you and to you, your eyewitness report of His goodness, the compound affect a moment of His attention makes in your life can change theirs as well.

That's why visitation is important. Visitation is a time and place where truth is clearly revealed in such a loving way that we are able to accept it, and that truth we accept can have its delivering and healing effect on our souls. In this place and during these times, we are able to look at the ugliest and most hurtful things in our lives without experiencing the irreconcilable pain of them. And as we look, the Lord applies the "Balm of Gilead"—His great love—and our wounds are cured forever. As this happens, He develops within us a "lovership" between our heart and His. Our souls are restored. Psalm 23 paints a beautiful picture of this process.

Let's look at Acts 3:

> *So repent (change your mind and purpose); turn around and return [to God], that your sins may be erased (blotted out, wiped clean), that times of refreshing (of recovering from the effects of heat, of reviving with fresh air) may come from the **presence** of the Lord; and that He may send [to you] the Christ (the Messiah), Who before was designated and appointed to you—even Jesus* Acts 3:19-20.

Remember, the word "presence" in this scripture is from a word that means "face" Strong's 4383:

- The face, the front of the human head, countenance, look, i.e., the face so far forth as it is the organ of sight, and by it various movements and changes; the index of the inward thoughts and feelings.

Do you see that? "The index of the inward thoughts and feelings." Pause and think about that. In His face—when we are face to face with Him—not only are we transparent before Him, as we always are, but, we have access to His inward thoughts and feelings. This is where our thoughts begin becoming aligned with His thoughts and our ways begin aligning with His ways.

⊷Refreshing comes when we are face to face with our Lord.

Face to face is also where our thoughts and feelings are exposed to us. Often we don't realize what we actually think or feel until we either talk with someone about it or it is revealed (indexed) to us in the presence of our Lord. When we talk about things with another person or persons, often we experience the feelings that accompany and undergird our understanding of it. As we re-experience these things they are imprinted more deeply on our souls and in our sub-conscious. Therefore, they are not resolved, rather are often, exacerbated instead. So they continue growing and festering.

Visitation—though it can be surprising, revelatory, exciting, or even funny—always changes us. Founded upon our relationship with the written Word of God, we develop . . .

> . . .*as with unveiled face, [because we] continued to behold [in the Word of God] as in a mirror the glory of the Lord, are constantly being transfigured into His very own image in ever increasing splendor and from one degree of glory to another; for this comes from the Lord [Who is] the Spirit* 2 Corinthians 3:18.

Time is the key to any relationship or endeavor. Every single thing we do involves an <u>investment</u> of our time. Until we can embrace the concept of eternity, our lives are measured by time. Therefore, in essence, when we spend time, we are investing our lives into that moment. A conscious and deliberate investment in face-to-face time with the living God, whether He presents

Himself to us as Father God, Jesus Christ, Holy Spirit or a combination, will deepen our relationship and understanding with the Trinity, the Three In One. Any time we spend in communion with God is an investment into "the heavenly stock of eternity."

During these times of refreshing, we will not only receive healing, particularly healing of the soul and maturing of our spirit, but we will also find that the more time we spend in that sanctified atmosphere, the more our thoughts and our ways will become aligned with the thoughts and ways of God.

David requested, *"Show me your ways, O Lord; teach me your paths"* Psalms 25:4. To Moses, God *"made known His ways"* Psalms 103:7. You see? Yes, His thoughts are above our thoughts and His ways above ours Isaiah 55:8-9, but He wants us to know His thoughts toward us Psalms 139:17, Jeremiah 29:11-14 and walk in His ways 1 Kings 3:14, 1 Kings 11:38, Zechariah 3:7.

David waged war, unified the nation and amassed great wealth and huge amounts of material for Solomon to build the Temple of God, all because of his personal relationship with God. He asked questions about what to do, how to do it and when it should be done. He wasn't perfect as we all know, but he had regular two-way conversations with the Lord. He sought the Lord's face and communed with Him.

All our battles are fought on the natural plane. The thing is, the consequences of the outcome of our inner battles are of utmost importance in the eternal plane and in the development of the Kingdom of Heaven on earth.

So, what are the qualifications to have face-to-face communion with the Living God? Perhaps John, Paul, and Peter have the answer:

Jesus answered, If a person [really] loves Me, he will keep My word [obey My teaching]; and My Father will love him, and We will come to him and make Our home (abode, special dwelling place) with him [John 14:23].

Do you not know that your body is the temple (the very sanctuary) of the Holy Spirit, Who lives within you, Whom you have received [as a Gift] from God? You are not your own. You were bought with a price [purchased with a preciousness and paid for, made His own]..... [1 Corinthians 6:19-20].

2 Peter 1:2-11: Peter instructs us in this passage and encourages to, *be all the more solicitous and eager to make sure (to ratify, to strengthen, to make steadfast) your calling and election, for if you do this,* you *will never stumble or fall. Thus there will be richly and abundantly provided for you entry into the eternal kingdom of our Lord and Savior Jesus Christ.*

So, if we are the special dwelling place, the very home of Jesus and Father God, AND a sanctuary or temple of Holy Spirit, we should begin reflecting the character of Those living within. The evidence, the fruit of the Spirit of God should begin to become obvious in our lives. Yes, it is a "beginning to become," because it's a lifelong process based upon ever increasing, ever deepening relationship. The fruit that reveals the indwelling Spirit of God and that should be demonstrated and clearly seen in our lives is . . .

love, joy (gladness), peace, patience/longsuffering [KJV] *(an even temper, forbearance), kindness, goodness (benevolence), faithfulness, gentleness (meekness, humility), self-control* ^{Galatians 5:22-23}.

Sometimes we try to change ourselves to change our nature ourselves. It seems the harder we try to "be good," the more we expose how imperfect we really are. The bearing of fruit is a work Holy Spirit accomplishes within us.

I discovered a note in The Open Bible, KJV, Note V(A), at bottom of page 1102, which helped me change my perspective and cease striving, trying to bear fruit. Let me share that with you:

The fruit of the Spirit is love, and it is manifested in joy, peace, long-suffering, gentleness, goodness, faith, meekness, temperance:

Joy is love's strength.

Peace is love's security.

Long-suffering is love's patience.

Gentleness is love's conduct.

Goodness is love's character.

Faith is love's confidence.

Meekness is love's humility.

Temperance is love's victory.

Against such there is no law.

A Holy Spirit-controlled man needs no law to cause him to live a righteous life.

If our hearts are filled with cold hearted, self-serving, hatred, bitterness, unforgiveness, envyings, guilt, resentment, suspicion, pride, manipulations, and/or other negative hurtful attitudes, it isn't the nature of Christ that's formed in us. It's the nature of satan. We need to be remodeled—renovated. 2 Peter gives us a step-by-step blueprint for this renovation.

May grace (God's favor) and peace (which is perfect well-being, all necessary good, all spiritual prosperity, and freedom from fears and agitating passions and moral conflicts) be multiplied to you in [the full, personal, precise, and correct] knowledge of God and of Jesus our Lord. For His divine power has bestowed upon us all things that [are requisite and suited] to life and godliness, through the [full, personal] knowledge of Him Who called us by and to His own glory and excellence (virtue). By means of these He has bestowed on us His precious and exceedingly great promises, so that through them you may escape [by flight] from the moral decay (rottenness and corruption) that is in the world because of covetousness (lust and greed) and become sharers (partakers) of the divine nature [2 Peter 1:2-4].

You see? God has given us everything we need to become partakers of the divine nature by knowing His Son and allowing Holy Spirit to form Christ in us. We have to choose if that's what we want. It's about truly knowing Him, not just knowing about Him. In one word—**Relationship**.

* * * * * * * * *

QUESTIONS and EXERCISES

1. Where are some places you feel the presence of the Lord?
2. Where do you go when you just want to be alone or when you MUST hear from God?
3. Visit your favorite place (in the spirit) and just begin praising the Lord, expecting Him to respond and to reveal Himself to you.
4. What is your understanding of habitation in reference to God—Father, Son and Holy Spirit—and you?
5. Continue mediating on the Word of God.
6. Regularly saturate yourself in worship.
7. Allow yourself to reach for relationship with the Most High God.

THE KINGDOM WITHIN

.....The Kingdom[1] of God[2] does not come with signs to be observed or with visible display, nor will people say, Look! Here [it is]! or, See, [it is] there! For behold, *the kingdom of God is within you, [in your hearts] and among you [surrounding you]*. Luke 17:20-21.

1. **Kingdom:** royal power, kingship, dominion, rule; not to be confused with an actual kingdom but rather the **right or authority to rule over a kingdom**.
2. **God**: spoken of the only and true God; refers to **the things of God; i.e., His counsels, interests, things due to Him**.
   Also: whatever can in any respect be likened unto God, or resemble Him in any way: **God's representative or vice-regent; of magistrates and judges.**

(Pause and think about the Kingdom of God with these amplifications in mind.)

Because **the Kingdom of God** (the right or authority to rule) is **within** us, we have the ability to form—to establish the Kingdom of Heaven **around** us. Jesus said in Matthew 10:7: . . . *as* *you go, preach, saying, The Kingdom of Heaven is at hand.* Part of what the phrase, *at hand*, means here is, "near or that the time is imminent and soon to come to pass."

Through the cross of Christ—the Blood of the Lamb—we have been given the right, the authority to rule on earth by/through the laws of heaven and the power of Holy Spirit. As we live in the Word and the Word lives in us, we are changed from glory to glory and should affect change wherever we go. When God has made Himself real to us, (the Kingdom of God **in** us) we establish the Kingdom of Heaven **around** us—we become world changers.

HEAVEN: the vaulted expanse of the sky with all things visible in it; the universe, the world; the aerial heavens or sky, the region where the clouds and the tempests gather, and where thunder and lightning are produced; the sidereal or starry heavens. The region above the sidereal heavens, **the seat of order of things eternal and consummately perfect** where God dwells and other heavenly beings.

Now, watch this. The Kingdom of Heaven is the same but works differently according to how/who we were created to be. The Lord explained it in ways everyone could understand:

.....The Kingdom of Heaven is like a grain of mustard seed, which a man took and sowed in his field Matthew 13:31.

(A farmer or gardener would understand this.)

....The Kingdom of Heaven is like leaven (sour dough) which a woman took and covered over in three measures of meal or flour till all of it was leavened Matthew 13:33.
(A cook – professional or domestic, a homemaker would understand this.)

The Kingdom of Heaven is like something precious buried

*in a field, which a man found and hid again; then in his
joy he goes and sells all he has and buys that field* ^{Matthew}
13:44.

(A geologist, archaeologist, an investment broker, a
collector of rare and valued objects would understand
this.)

*Again the Kingdom of Heaven is like a man who is a
dealer in search of fine and precious pearls, who, on
finding a single pearl of great price, went and sold all he
had and bought it* ^{Matthew 13:45-46}.

(An investment broker, jeweler, a collector of rare gems,
a collector of beauty would understand this.)

*Again, the Kingdom of Heaven is like a dragnet, which
was cast into the sea, and gathered in fish of every sort*
Matthew 13:47.

(A fisherman – domestic, sport or someone feeding his
family would understand this.)

*He said to them, Therefore every teacher and interpreter
of the Sacred Writings who has been instructed about and
trained for the kingdom of heaven and has become a
disciple is like a householder who **brings forth** out of his
storehouse **treasure that is new and [treasure that is] old
[the fresh as well as the familiar]*** ^{Matthew 13:52}.

(Teachers, Homeowners, Parents, Merchants, Preachers,
Researchers and Librarians would understand this.)

I really like the above verse, #52. If we are trained for the
Kingdom and become a disciple, our job description as
described in this verse states that we are to bring forth new
treasure (revelation) and continue teaching the familiar or
foundational things as well.

- **New** as respects form: superior to what it succeeds.
- **New** as respects substance: unprecedented, uncommon, unheard of.

Whatever it is you were created and appointed to be—that's how you will see and understand the Kingdom of God. So give yourself permission to see and be according to your call. Don't try to be like someone else or like people seem to expect you to be. Embrace the position God made you to fill, the assignment He put you on earth to accomplish. It's okay to be a farmer even if your family line is packed with successful merchants.

The mysteries of the Word of God are being revealed from generation to generation. The Living Word is so exciting! The more we learn, the more there is to know and understand—as we grow fuller The Word grows deeper! I love His Word!

And as you go, preach, saying, "The Kingdom of Heaven is at hand" Matthew 10:7!

- The amplification of the phrase "at hand," indicates that phrase also means to bring near, to join one thing to another, to draw or come near to, to approach.
  - o As Holy Spirit brings us near, our consciousness is joined to Him. We become less self conscious and more God conscious. We learn to be led of the Spirit rather than being led by our soulish desires and impulses.
  - o The Spirit of God within each of us draws others to desire to know Jesus, to join the Kingdom of Heaven through salvation.
  - o The kingdoms of our heart are joined to the Kingdom of our dear Lord.

- o **Thus the phrase, "at hand," indicates a total transformation of each individual and their area of influence.**

Let's look at a few more scriptures.

But you are not living the life of the flesh, you are living the life of the Spirit, if the [Holy] Spirit of God [really] dwells within you [directs and controls you]. . . Romans 8:9 *.*

*Do you not discern and understand that you are God's temple (His sanctuary), and that **God's Spirit has His permanent dwelling in you** [to be at home in you, collectively as a church and also individually]?* 1 Corinthians 3:16 *.*

*Judas, not Iscariot, asked Him, Lord, how is it that You will reveal Yourself [**make Yourself real**] to us and not to the world?* John 14:22 *.*

Remember Jesus' response? He said, "Father and I will come live in you."

Isn't that interesting and amazing? God—Father, Son and Holy Spirit—wants relationship <u>with us</u>. **They actually move toward us first, They draw near to us.** (*We love Him because He first loved us and gave Himself for us* 1 John 14:19 *.*) It's as though He takes a step forward and extends His hand to us all we have to do is reach out and take it. If we obey His teaching, allow His Word to live in us and we live in His Word, He and the Father will join Holy Spirit <u>in us,</u> making us their special dwelling. **Jesus will make Himself real to us** John 14:21-23 *.*

In this [union and communion with Him] love is brought to completion and attains perfection with us, that we may *have confidence for the day of judgment [with assurance and boldness to face Him], because **as He is, so are we in this world** [1 John 4:17].*

Selah! Pause and think about that!
And – this.

*The wind blows (breathes) where it <u>wills</u>; and though you hear its sound, yet you neither know where it comes from nor where it is going. **So it is with everyone who is born of the Spirit** [John 3:8].*

- **Wills** (listeth *KJV*): To be resolved or determined, to purpose, to desire, to wish, to love; to like to do a thing, be fond of doing, to take delight in, have pleasure.

So, now we know that the wind does not blow undirected. Its blowing is purposeful, determined, is full of delight and pleasure. We also learn that **we are like the wind if we are in the Spirit, not in the flesh.** And remember, **"as He is so are we in this world"** [1 John 4:17]!

SELAH – Pause and think about that again!!!

Oh! To have full understanding of that one phrase! It could change the world.

When we read the Word of God, gain understanding of what it means, then apply that understanding to the way we conduct our lives, His Word lives in us. Through this process we begin living in Him, doing, saying and thinking in line with how He does, says and thinks. Then, His place within us is enlarged, His Kingdom is expanded.

Consider these scriptures:

[After all] the kingdom of God is not a matter of getting the food and drink one likes, but instead is righteousness (that state which makes a person acceptable to God) and [heart] peace and joy in the Holy Spirit Romans 14:17.

And [besides] we ourselves have seen (have deliberately and steadfastly contemplated) and bear witness that the Father has sent the Son [as the] Savior of the world. Anyone who confesses (acknowledges, owns) that Jesus is the Son of God, God abides (lives, makes His home) in him and he [abides, lives, makes his home] in God. And we know (understand, recognize, are conscious of, by observation and by experience) and believe (adhere to and put faith in and rely on) the love God cherishes for us. God is love, and he who dwells and continues in love dwells and continues in God and God dwells and continues in him 1 John 4:14-16.

Take another look at 1 John 4:17-18:

In this [union and communion with Him] love is brought to completion and attains perfection with us, that we may have confidence for the day of judgment [with assurance and boldness to face Him], because as He is, so are we in this world. There is no fear in love [dread does not exist], but full-grown (complete, perfect) love turns fear out of doors and expels every trace of terror. For fear brings with it the thought of punishment, and [so] **he who is afraid has not reached the full maturity of love** *(is not yet grown into love's complete perfection).*

Many of us pray for boldness. I have been guilty of this many times, I have actually begged for boldness. Most of us do not realize that boldness is an outgrowth of LOVE! (I didn't.) When love is "full grown," fear of rejection, fear of man, fear of any nature flees. Our boldness is not objectionable because when we move and speak in love, the tone of our voice, the look in our eyes, even the color of our countenance is changed to reflect the One we represent. People hear, see, and experience Jesus when love is full grown in us.

Oh, that we would all come to that place where we so trust and love God that we would be able to lay aside every trace of fear. If we could banish every mal thought and demolish the walls of suspicion and prejudice, the love God has shed abroad in our hearts could flow like a refreshing river to those around us. Healing and restoration of this world would leap forward and redemption would spring forth. The kingdoms of this world would become the Kingdoms of our dear Lord. Visitation would truly turn to Habitation. God—Father, Son and Holy Spirit—would be "made real" to the world.

Look closely at yourself in the mirror. Be kindhearted toward who you see and you will recognize Him, the Lord, reflected through your eyes.

****

QUESTIONS and EXERCISES

1. Enter into worship.
   a. Soft instrumental worship music can help detach from the distractions of the world so we are able to release ourselves to His presence.
2. Ask the Lord to show you the Kingdom within.
   a. Write down what you are shown and review it from time to time. You will see the Kingdom grow within you and become established around you as your understanding and knowledge of Him grows and deepens.

LIVING BEYOND THE BOOK

If the Bible were being compiled today,
How many modern-day ministers and martyrs
Would be found in its pages?

This chapter is titled "Living Beyond the Book" simply to open our minds to see the fact that those whose lives are detailed in the Bible did not have the scriptures to base their lives on. As a matter of fact, their lives are the foundation of scripture. There is a saying for which I do not know the source. It goes like this. "In the Old the New is concealed. In the New the Old is revealed." 1 Corinthians 10:11, speaking of the Old Testament, tells us:

Now these things befell them by way of a figure [as an example and warning to us]; they were written to admonish and fit us for right action by good instruction, we in whose days the ages have reached their climax (their consummation and concluding period).

That word "figure" here, "ensamples" in the King James Version, means examples, but it also means warnings. The examples of what people did right as well as what they did wrong, form the boundaries of our guidelines. Those "ensamples" from the

Old Testament were written specifically for those who lived in the New Testament and for us. Fortunately, we have the New Testament, the New Covenant, to teach us to live eternally with Jesus as our example. His life shows us we can trust God in every situation.

We, today, have the advantage of knowing, being able to review, the successes and failures of those in the Old Testament and those whose lives are revealed in the New Testament. The New Testament reveals the New Covenant which is called a "better covenant," because it is ratified by the blood of God's only begotten Son rather than the blood of bulls and goats [Jeremiah 31:31-34, Hebrews 8:6-13]. Until very recently, animal sacrifices have not been made during the Jewish celebrations since the Cross of Christ.

The Words God spoke and the deeds God did have been carefully recorded for our edification. As we study the experiences of people whose lives are recorded in the Bible and learn the principles that determined the outcome of their lives, we embrace truths that can guide us around pitfalls in our own lives. We need to apply the principles laid out as guidelines to our natural and spiritual development. He is no respecter of persons. His Word has gone forth and must perform what it was sent to do. When we are able to own it for ourselves—He will do for us as surely as He did for those written about. He will honor His Word in our lives.

During the days of the Old Covenant a handful of men and a few women saw and conversed with angels, heard God, even saw and talked with the Lord. God's actual plan and His desire was that all draw near to Him [Deuteronomy 5:22-28]. But, many were and are afraid. However, it is not the drawing near we should fear. Rather, we should fear disobedience. We should fear rebellion. We should fear taking His concepts and precepts lightly. We should fear not developing an intimate, personal relationship with the Living God. We should be aware of and fear the possibility of eternity sealed from His presence—an eternity of torment in a loveless dark place with no hope of redemption.

We are told in Job, Psalms and Proverbs, that *the fear of the Lord is the beginning of wisdom.* We need to "begin" in wisdom and continue therein, pursuing it as we pursue life itself. As we gain understanding of His ways and His great love for us, we are able to run boldly to Him because His love is perfected in us. Perfect love casts out all fear.

Often those who do not know Him ask how a loving God could condemn people to such a fate as hell. He is not the one who condemns us. He allowed His only begotten Son sacrificed in a hideous and shameful way to save us from that fate of darkness. Our own choices condemn us, or lead us to redemption. If even with our last breath we choose the sacrificial gift of the cross, God honors that choice and welcomes us into eternal arms of love just as surely as He honored the thief on the cross [Luke 23:42-43].

Deuteronomy 30:19 tells us:

> *I call heaven and earth to witness this day against you that I have set before you life and death, the blessings and the curses; therefore choose life that you and your descendants may live and may love the Lord your God, obey His voice, and cling to Him. For He is your life and the length of your days, that you may dwell in the land which the Lord swore to give to your fathers, to Abraham, Isaac and Jacob.*

Consider the possibility that your testimony—your life—could become the bright light that shines through the darkness of someone's world revealing another choice—a better way. Does your life display enough godly principles to draw others to explore the possibilities of life in Christ? Does mine?

<u>Living beyond the Book is all about living in Christ.</u>

Living in Christ means:
- Living a life as partakers of the divine nature.
- Living a life that draws others to choose life.
- Absorbing the written Word, the Bible, applying its precepts and concepts to our lives.
- Letting our lives and minds be changed as Christ is formed in us.
- Living in such a way that we are not simply taking up space, or worse, adding to the problems of society, but rather being a force for good.
- Changing the atmosphere we occupy to reflect the Kingdom of Heaven as we obey God's commands and live by His precepts.
- Living in Christ is "living beyond the Book."

The Book (The Bible):
- Contains everything needed to lead us to salvation.
- Gives us step by step instructions to mature spiritually to the point of living a holy life.
- Instructs us in how to become partakers of the divine nature.
- Contains the wisdom to raise our children in the admonition of the Lord.
- Gives precise instructions to apply wisdom to gain financial prosperity.
- Contains all the direction we need to choose the proper mate and develop successful marriages.
- Teaches us how to maintain good relationships with our neighbors.

- Instructions us in the building and maintaining healthy communities.
- Contains war strategies as well as how to live in peace with our enemies.
- Shows us how to develop and maintain relationships with mankind, angels and the holy, eternal, living God.
- Instructs us in ways to resist the temptations of our flesh and escape the corruption of this world.
- Instructs us in ways to defeat the enemy of our souls—the devil—the enemy of our Maker.

If no other books were written on any of our foundational instructions concerning living a successful from birth to eternity life, the Bible would be enough.

THE BIBLE IS TRULY A LIVING BOOK:
- Every time we read it we find something new.
  - This is because as we grow and mature our understanding deepens so we "see" things we couldn't see and understand before.
  - We are able to understand to a greater depth the truths we learned previously.
  - It actually seems the Bible grows <u>with</u> us though the "new" information was there all along. We just couldn't see it.

Here's the thing. God did not stop talking to mankind when the first "Bible"—the Holy Scriptures—was compiled. For some, the portion we know as the "Old Testament" contains <u>all</u> the "divine" writings. The Jews break it down to the Torah, the Pentateuch, Septuagint and the Prophets.

Others embrace only the New Testament. They believe the "old" was done away with by the Cross of Christ which closed the door on the "old" covenant ratified only by the blood of bulls and goats and replaced it with the better or, New Covenant ratified by the Blood of God's own Son. Though this may be fundamentally true [Jeremiah 31:31-33; Hebrews 8-9, 12:24], it does not embrace the whole truth. Jesus Himself said that neither jot nor tittle (the smallest grammatical mark nor the smallest stroke of a Hebrew letter) would pass from the law—become unimportant.

There are also those who embrace the writings between the Old and New Testaments called The Mccabees. Others of us don't know what The Mccabees are. This brings us to those of us who embrace the "Whole Word."

I personally believe the Bible contains everything necessary to life—both natural and eternal. I also believe there are many sermons, lessons and anointed books written by current ministers and authors, which, if subjected to the tests of canonization would be selected as divine revelation and included in the Bible were it being compiled today.

God is always communicating with mankind. The angels were not fired nor retired on the day of Pentecost when man was consummated by Holy Spirit. Experiences recorded in the Bible give us a standard to judge and prove the revelations and encounters people are sharing today.

Consider this: Our lives are books being read by everyone with whom we come in contact. Just as the first disciples of Jesus wrote about their experiences with and because of Him, so our lives reflect our relationship with Him as well.

Living beyond the Book is not being conformed to or by the principles of this world but being transformed by the renewing of our minds [Romans 12:2].

In 2 Peter 1:2-11, Peter is praying that God's grace and

peace be multiplied to us in a more excellent knowledge of God and of Jesus. He further tells us that God's divine power has given us everything we need to live a godly life. This power operates in us through our personal relationship with Jesus. He has called us by and to His own glory and excellence through which He has honored us with exceedingly great promises we do not deserve. Because of this, we are able to escape the moral decay and corruption that is in the world. He tells us we can even become partakers or sharers of the divine nature.

Peter gives us a blueprint to advance in our spiritual development:

- God has given us divine promises to which we are to add diligence. In other words, we are not to neglect those promises but begin building our lives around and upon them.
- Then we are to employ every effort in exercising our faith to develop virtue which is excellence, resolution and Christian energy.
- In exercising this virtue we develop knowledge or intelligence.
- In exercising intelligence we develop self control.
- In exercising self-control develop steadfastness which is patience and endurance.
- In exercising steadfastness we develop godliness.
- In exercising godliness we develop brotherly affection.
- In exercising brotherly affection we develop Christian love.
  - As these qualities develop in us, our personal knowledge of Jesus Christ becomes full and fruitful.
  - If we don't develop these qualities we are spiritually shortsighted, blinded to the truth of salvation. We become cold and lose hope, forgetting that we have been cleansed from our old sins.

- Because it is possible to become blind, cold and without hope, we are to eagerly strengthen, ratify and make steadfast our calling and election—our choice of salvation and development through Jesus Christ.
  - If we these steps, we won't stumble or fall and there will be richly and abundantly provided for us entry into the eternal Kingdom of our Lord and Savior Jesus Christ.

IN CHRIST is how we do the GREATER WORKS!

I assure you, most solemnly I tell you, if anyone steadfastly believes in Me, he will himself be able to do the things that I do and he will do even greater things than these; because I go to My Father [John 14:12].

* * * * * * * * *

EXERCISES

1. The triune God lives within you. Commune with Him, purposefully enter into His presence daily.
2. Allow your heart to reach for Him.
3. Keep a journal of the work of the Spirit in your life as you continue pressing into visitation and toward habitation.
4. How has visitation changed you thus far?

PRACTICAL APPLICATION

As we participate in the Kingdom of God within us it begins growing – expanding outward, establishing the Kingdom of Heaven around us.

As we read the example of the Children of Israel in Deuteronomy 5:22-28, we see that the Lord God wants us ALL to draw close. He truly wants us to come boldly to the throne of grace [Hebrews 4:16], because He is familiar with exactly what we go through on earth and has been touched and tempted in every respect, as we are [Hebrews 4:15]. So, as we come boldly before the throne of God, we receive mercy, grace, and help just when we need it [Hebrews 4:16].

- He paid the price to reconcile us with the Father.
  - A price too often taken for granted.
  - A great price that purchased rights and privileges we often give little thought to and all too often are actually unaware of.
  - The Cross of Christ reopened communications between mankind and the eternal, living God.
  - More than that, the Cross of Christ brings us into family relationship with the Creator of the universe, the Creator of all things—the created to the Creator.

- He longs for us to come to Him:
  - As children to their loving Father.
  - As brides to their bridegroom.
  - As intimate friends.

Take Note: Not one person who was waiting in the Upper Room on the day of Pentecost failed to receive and be filled by Holy Spirit. They were not perfect people. They were made acceptable by the Gift of God, wrapped in flesh and tied with the ribbon of the cross.

As we practice His presence, we develop that open communication that permits us to run to Papa, climb up in His lap and hug His neck, just as we would pick up the phone and call our mom, or simply pop into our parents' home unannounced. Sometimes there is protocol. Sometimes He simply wants us to run to Him crying, "Abba!" "Father!"

He's always with us, *all the days (perpetually, uniformly, and on every occasion), to the very close and consummation of the age* ^{Matthew 28:20}.

Daily practicing His presence—being purposely aware of Him, is the way we develop continual communion with Him. This continual communion will bring us through inner/emotional healing and deliverance, as well as endue us with direction, discernment, inexplicable compassion, great mercy, discretion and uncommon love. It will position us to be in the right place at the right time to:

- Avoid mistakes.
- Receive blessings.
- Speak a word in season.
- Save a life.
- Offer salvation.

- Meet someone with the key to our destiny.
- Meet someone for whom we have or are the key to their destiny.

Continual communion is the way we learn to hear the still small voice that says, *"This is the way, walk in it"* Isaiah 30:21.

It has been my experience that the Lord began preparing most of us while we were still children. There was a particular place where we felt safe and happy; a place where we experienced the love of the living God, whether we recognized it as that or not.

- For me it was the woods of Arkansas.
- For Fran it was a large rock in a neighbor's yard.*
- For Novella it was her Grandmother's house.*
- For Diana it was her Grandparents house.*
- For you it may be the beach or the mountains.
- It may be when you're hidden in your closet, on the rooftop, or on your patio.
- He told the disciples to pull away privately after ministering Luke 9:10.
- Even Jesus pulled away privately to commune with Father.
  - First to the wilderness Matthew 3:16, 14:23.
  - After the feeding of the 5,000 men plus women and children Matthew 14:23, John 6:15.
  - To the Mount of Olives John 8:1.

Find your place or places of communion. Remember the experience of that place and begin practicing His presence. He will not disappoint you. It isn't the same for everyone and it will vary from time to time for each of us. I have experienced angels coming for me and taking me to Him. I have experienced flying by myself. I have been "snatched away" by the Spirit. I have experienced the Lord rending the heavens and coming for me.

These things have happened unexpectedly as well as when I purposely positioned myself for visitation. They have happened when I was in the secret place, or at work, walking down the hall, while driving or riding in a car, during praise, when I was deeply hurt, when I was ecstatically happy, when I was alone, when I was with others, when I was thinking of Him and when I wasn't. Even when I have been angry with Him, He still communed with me drawing me to trust. (I don't recommend being angry with Him— there can be harsh consequences. I'm just telling you in such times, He still loves us and is still willing to appear to us and talk with us.)

There is no set pattern or required components other than a desire to know Him. He will come to us even when we don't recognize that longing we are experiencing is a heart cry for communion with Him. However Psalm105:1-5 is a very good place to begin:

O Give thanks unto the Lord, call upon His name, make known His doings among the peoples!

Sing to Him, sing praises to Him; meditate on and talk of all His marvelous deeds and devoutly praise them.

Glory in His holy name; let the hearts of those rejoice who seek and require the Lord [as their indispensable necessity].

Seek, inquire of and for the Lord and crave Him and His strength (His might and inflexibility to temptation); seek and require His face and His presence [continually] evermore.

Earnestly remember the marvelous deeds that He has done, His miracles and wonders, the judgments and sentences which He pronounced [upon His enemies, as in Egypt].

Seek Him with all your heart. Allow yourself to long for Him—for even, just a glimpse of Him. Live in His Word. Think on and meditate on His Word until it lives in you and you live in it.

- Expect Him to show up in board meetings, in the park, on the freeway, in your bedroom or in the kitchen.
- Expect Him to show up in church and in your secret place.
- Expect Him to wake you in the middle of the night.
- Expect to hear His voice when you have questions or when you've been pondering or meditating.
- He has the answers you need.
- Expect and allow Him to participate in your everyday life.

EXPECT HIM!

What I call "visitation" some people call ascending. To ascend is to rise, climb, soar, go up, or come up. I believe ascending can be a part of it—the very special part where we are able to lay aside everything else and enter that realm. But He is an "every day, every way" God. He will surprise us in the most unexpected times, places and ways.

**As we participate in the Kingdom of God within us
it begins growing, expanding outward
as it establishes The Kingdom,
the rule or government of Heaven around us.**

* * * * * * * * *

EXERCISE

1. Begin training your senses to <u>expect</u> to hear His voice and to see His face.
2. Pray in the Spirit every chance you have, without ceasing as Paul suggests [1 Thessalonians 5:17].

3. When you have a question, expect and wait for His answer. Even at work or in meetings, you have time to hear from Him.
4. Practice His presence every chance you get. He is talking to you.
5. Develop the habit of expectation. Then move forward into acceptance of His presence with you and His great love for you.
6. Become continually aware of the Kingdom of God within you.
7. At every opportunity – purposely demonstrate the principles of the Kingdom of God, establishing the Kingdom wherever you are.
8. Be a billboard for Kingdom Principles!

FROM VISITATION
TO
HABITATION

It's not a matter of "doing"
It's a matter of "being".

We are all familiar with some of the lives and incidents that will be discussed in this chapter. However, perhaps we have not looked at them from this viewpoint—the viewpoint of God's great love for us and His Kingdom being established as Heaven meets Earth.

The first instance, of course, is in the Garden of Eden. God walked with Adam and Eve. The earth did not shake. There was no smoke. There was no fire. There was no thunder and lightning. God walked on earth with man and talked with them. He didn't have to do that. He could have simply watched them and talked with them from heaven. BUT!!! He wanted relationship!

Telegraph, telephone, television, tell-a-person, e-mail, texting, video conferencing, Face Book, Youtube and all the other forms of communication are wonderful. But true, intimate relationship can only be built in the express presence of one another, face-to-face. God purposely set that pattern into the substance of the Garden with Adam and Eve. He wants face-to-face relationship with us so love can grow. All the other forms of communication plant seeds for intimacy. Those seeds sprout and bear fruit when we are face-to-face—in the presence of one another.

When we are in the presence of another person, face-to-face, communication transmission is multiplied by our senses. Let's bring this into first person. When I am face-to-face with someone, I know they are connecting to and communicating directly with me. I not only hear their voice, I see their facial expression and know they are communing with me. I can "read" between the words and see their heart in the matter being discussed. I can see if they're at peace, angry, distraught, happy, sad, worried, or curious. I look into their eyes and know they are looking into me. I notice their body language—whether they are relaxed or defensive, perhaps reaching out to me or needing me to reach out to them. I sense their emotions and know my presence is affecting them as their presence affects me. They can actually "see" my intentions not just hear my words.

Presence is very powerful in various way and multiple levels of "being."Sometimes, just sitting silently with someone strengthens you as well as them.

It's easy to be misunderstood on the phone, especially if one is in a hurry or the situation is tense. And e-mail and/or texting! How cold is that?! Many relationships have been injured—even destroyed—by misunderstanding e-mail and texting. But when we are in the presence of one another—face to face—intent can be understood, emotions tasted, true caring confirmed and intimacy developed.

Many of us are unaware that God—Father, Son and Holy Spirit—wants that type relationship with us. We may have intellectual knowledge of this yet not grasp that such intimacy with the triune God is actually possible. We've been taught more about fearing the devils and avoiding the supernatural at all cost than we've been taught about the beauty of the love of God.

In truth, we don't have to slay dragons, live in the slums of poverty, subdue vile nations, chain the devil or be pure as the driven snow to be "good enough" for divine relationship. The most important thing is to understand the possibilities for friendship and desire to know God. He's not out to get us! He created us for relationship and went so far as to suffer shame, rejection, misunderstanding and death—cruel and indescribably tortuous—just to make the way clear for us to "come close."

Let's take another look at Adam and Eve. One thing that surprised me when I finally saw it during my umpteenth reading of this portion of scripture was that God did not withhold His PRESENCE from them when they were shut out of the Garden. I knew He still talked with them, but I hadn't considered His presence. It wasn't just His voice floating down from Heaven; He was still with them, communicating and available for relationship. It's the same for us today. He is ever present with us [Matthew 28:20]. Let's take a closer look at Cain.

But for Cain and his offering He (God) had no respect or regard. So Cain was exceedingly angry and indignant and he looked sad and depressed. And the Lord said to Cain, Why are you angry? And why do you look sad and depressed and dejected? If you do well, will you not be accepted? And if you do not do well, sin crouches at your door; its desire is for you, but you must master (rule over, have dominion over) it [Genesis 4:5-7].

Cain reminds me of one of my brothers. When he was young (in his teens) and did something wrong, our dad would talk to him about it. My brother would hang his head (as many of us do) and not look into Daddy's eyes. He couldn't see the love in Daddy's eyes because he refused to look. I can see Cain doing just that. Cain didn't ask, "How? How do I master sin?" He probably knew. He had offered a "first fruit's offering" when he should have brought a sin offering. Without the shedding of blood there is no redemption for sin [Hebrews 9:22]. Unlike Cain, my brother responded when He heard the audible voice of the Lord. Thank God, the blood sacrifice has been made for us through the shedding of the Blood of His Own Son [Hebrews 9:23-26].

Here's my point regarding Cain and the presence of God:

The root meanings of the word sin include, "to miss oneself, lose oneself, wander from the way." Cain lived in the very presence of the Lord God but lost himself and wandered away. How different this experience could have been had he looked into the Lord eyes and said, "I'm so sorry. Please forgive me. Let me now offer a blood sacrifice and I won't let this happen again." I believe he had that opportunity. But instead, he went out with hatred and murder in his heart and killed his brother. Now—sin had a firm grip on Cain and he was banished to Nod, the land of wandering.

So Cain went away from the presence of the LORD, and dwelt in the land of Nod (wandering), on the east of Eden
Genesis 4:16
.

Surprise! The Lord God's presence wasn't over all the Earth. Cain went away from the presence, the face, of the Lord.

God's presence is still with us today and manifests in "impossible" ways, at the most unexpected times and places.

Everything is held together and operates through the power of His Word [Hebrews 1:3, 11:3]. His influence even reaches into every nook and cranny of the universe places where life as we know it doesn't exist. A popular saying when I was growing up was, "You can run, but you can't hide." Psalm 139 amplifies that saying in verses 8 and 9:

If I ascend up into heaven, You are there; if I make my bed in Sheol (the place of the dead), behold, You are there.

There are multiple proofs of His presence recorded in scripture, as well as in the experiences of people throughout the world. Not only can I relate my own experiences, but listen to or read Dale Fife, Chuck Pierce, Paul Keith Davis, Heidi Bakker, James Goll, Wendy Alec, Paul Cox, Barbara Wentroble, Sid Roth—Oh My! The list goes on and on and includes thousands of people I have never heard of. There are even reports of people in non-Christian nations coming to know the Lord because of an audible voice or a manifestation of His presence. But, I know we all like proof and scriptural confirmation. Let's look at a few more instances from the Bible.

Noah heard God's voice and followed His plan to preserve "seeds" for a new beginning on Earth. Noah's assignment took several years to complete. He didn't make excuses—he just got down to business. God had found Noah to be perfect in his generations. Yet—God did not dwell in Noah.

God spoke to Abraham when he was still a pagan known as Abram, telling him to leave everything and almost everyone he knew. The Lord visited Abram in person from time to time. One time, He brought two companions with Him, angels on assignment to destroy a couple of towns. Why did the Lord and His companions manifest their presence to Abram? Because God considered him to be a friend with whom He should share His plans for the immediate future as well as His plan for generations to come.

God had a plan to use Abram; a plan to develop a people He could use as examples of His great love and watch-care over mankind. This is the root of our relationship with God even to this day ^{Romans 4:16, 9:7-8}[Romans 4:16, 9:7-8]. We who believe in Christ and accept Him as our personal Lord and Savior have entered into the promise given to Abraham and have become fruit of that promise. We have entered into Christ thereby having our souls washed in His blood. We have been grafted into the Promise and become sons and daughters of Abraham, grafted into the commonwealth of Israel [Ephesians 2]. Though God called him "friend," God did not dwell in Abraham.

Following the experience with the bush that burned with fire, but was not consumed, Moses communed with God continually. He talked with God, argued with Him, even bargained with Him for the lives of the Children of Israel. Yet, God called Moses to the top of a mountain to speak with him. Once the Tabernacle was built, God visited with Moses and the Priests by means of a golden box called the Ark of the Covenant. Yes, in that time God did speak to various individuals by the Spirit as well as through angels. He also made His presence known by the cloud during day and the fire by night. Yet—God did not dwell in Moses.

God did not dwell in Daniel, Hananiah (Shadrach), Mishael (Meshach), or Azariah, (Abednego). He didn't inhabit any of the High Priests. He didn't make His special abode in Samuel, Deborah, Joshua, Jeremiah, Isaiah, Ezekiel, Zechariah, Elijah, Elisha, or even Enoch or the great King David.

*   *   *

We could run through every person named in the Bible from the closing of the Garden of Eden to a young girl named

Mary. She was the first to be a habitation of God. It wasn't the same as for us since the Cross of Christ—she carried the Holy Seed of God. Imagine the experiences of Joseph and Mary raising a child who embodied the Spirit of the Living God from conception! Even still, Jesus went off by Himself to commune with God.

After the Cross—then came Pentecost!

The word pentecost actually means, fifty or fiftieth day. For the most part it is connected with harvest. Fifty days after Passover, every family, brought two loaves of bread and two lambs to be sacrificed. No one was to eat of the harvest nor were first fruits offerings allowed until after the day of Pentecost.

In the exodus from Egypt, the people were dedicated to God as being first fruits. At Sinai their consecration to Him as a nation was completed fifty days—Pentecost—following their exodus. This was the time of the giving of the Law—the Ten Commandments—on Mount Sinai.

(Information concerning Pentecost was taken from Candlelight Software, Lexicon.)

It was fifty days—Pentecost—after the crucifixion that Holy Spirit came to those in the upper room like a rushing mighty wind, settling upon them with the appearance of tongues of fire! MANKIND BECAME TEMPLES OF THE LIVING GOD!!!

When our minds are set on God and the things of God, we become an open portal for heaven to come to earth.

The Kingdom of Heaven is established around us transforming Earth.
Hell recedes.
Wherever we go, that portal goes and lives are changed.

*   *   *

I was doing spiritual warfare over a town in Texas. At one point, my assistant and I were on our way to a meeting in a rural area. We had to pass a bar our team made proclamations over. It was known for prostitution, drug dealing and, of course, various other forms of immorality. We had bound demons from going into that place. We also bound those resident within the building so they could not leave nor could they influence people who went there. This was done in this manner because the Lord had not yet given us directions as to how we were to deal with them. The method and timing had to be in accordance with His everlasting plan for redeeming the land not just the building. Waiting on His direction and timing would close the gate/portal to hell that gave the demons access to this realm in that area. The bar soon closed for lack of business.

As we approached the area where the bar was we saw hundreds of demons of various sizes and shapes standing in the parking lot of the bar and spilling out onto the highway and into the field across the road from the bar. They covered the highway for a distance of about an eighth of a mile and were just standing looking toward the building. We could see other demons trapped inside peering out of the windows.

Fortunately, there was no traffic because when we saw the demons, we slowed down so we could take it all in. When they saw us, they began backing up off the highway, making a space for us to pass. Certainly, we could have driven right through them; I'm sure many vehicles did without the occupants even seeing them. God revealed their presence to us so we would know for certain our work was not in vain. The Kingdom of God was in, and with us, surrounding us. The "rule and governmental authority of heaven" was in us and on us.

Though the Lord had not yet told us what to do with or about those demons, they knew we had authority over them. Later my team and I went back to that building. We performed prophetic acts as directed by Holy Spirit. By the end of summer there was a successful secondhand business established there.

None of this was done through intellectual tactics or physical prowess. Everything we did in the battle for that town was done under the direction of Holy Spirit and backed up by heaven. Through a nine month siege on the kingdom of darkness under the direction of Holy Spirit, that town was changed. The ministerial alliance became a force for good and a symbol of unity for Kingdom establishment. The economy changed and the town long known as a place that bankrupted millionaires and where a large number of the population were physically disabled became a place of and prosperity, healing, and peace.

This wasn't just a bunch of women getting together for a little prayer meeting. It was about getting the strategy of heaven. It was about being willing to do strange and unfamiliar things (prophetic acts) before these types of things were common or comfortable. The Kingdom of God within us (the authority to rule) created the Kingdom of heaven around us.

Do you understand?

We are warring for heaven and Earth to become one.

*   *   *

The first time I experienced a place that had become completely consecrated to the Lord was February of 2000, when the Lord sent me to a conference I didn't want to attend. I was already registered for a conference in Oklahoma for that week.

In December of 1999, while I was praying for direction for the coming year, the Lord told me to "pursue wisdom."

"Lord, what do you mean? I've pursued wisdom all my life."

"No, You've sought wisdom. It's time to pursue and apprehend," was His reply.

"O.K. How do I start pursuing?"

"Attend the Winter Wisdom Conference," He instructed. (I had received an advertisement about it just a few days prior to this conversation.)

"Lord, that's the same week as the prophetic conference in Oklahoma City. I'm already registered for that. It's a week-long event and goes through the weekend." (I told Him this just in case He had forgotten or overlooked this little detail. 'Smile.')

The Lord didn't seem to care that I had already paid the registration fee and arranged for a place to stay in Oklahoma. He had a different plan for me. We as Christians need to get passed the idea that God never goes against our will. Until we surrender our will to Him and there is no longer this kind of battle, He will pursue us aggressively, or woo us tenderly until we relent.

I did go to the conference in Oklahoma. But, I drove back to Texas on Thursday evening so I could attend the weekend conference at the Wisdom Center. The next morning I left home early because I didn't know where the town was, let alone how I would find the Wisdom Center once I got there. (This was before GPS.) I arrived early, about an hour before Dr. Murdock arrived. Of course, his staff was there and as soon as they opened the building, I went inside.

Love saturated the atmosphere. It was palpable. Not only did I feel love soothing my emotions, I could smell love's fragrance. I could taste the sweetness of God. Love regenerated my strength. I could touch it with my fingers and see it in the air. This was a dimension of God I had not even imagined. Earth's love had not been kind to me, but this was different. I was there to pursue wisdom but I discovered the love of God. This was an outpost of heaven. Dr. Murdock had pulled heaven down to earth and established it in his church.

I didn't know Dr. Murdock, still don't. But, God knew him and he knew God. He had developed a lovership with the Holy Spirit I have experienced in only a handful of people. Had I not attended that meeting, I may never have known the depth of relationship God has made available to us. I was there to learn how to pursue wisdom. I discovered that the first step toward wisdom is to develop a lovership with the Lord. *Christ has been made Wisdom to us* [1 Corinthians 1:30]. *Christ is the power of God and the wisdom of God* [1 Corinthians 1:30]. Paul prays for the Christians at Ephesus: [*For I always pray to] the God of our Lord Jesus Christ, the Father of glory, that He may grant you a spirit of wisdom and revelation [of insight into mysteries and secrets] in the [deep and intimate] knowledge of Him* [Ephesians 1:17]. Lord, please grant this to me.

In Colossians 3:16, we are admonished to:

> *Let the word [spoken by]Christ (the Messiah) have its home [in your hearts and minds] and dwell in you in [all its] richness, as you teach and admonish and train one another* in all insight and intelligence and wisdom [in spiritual things, and as you sing] *psalms and hymns and spiritual songs , making melody to God with His grace in your hearts. And whatever you do [no matter what it is] in word or deed, do everything in the name of the Lord Jesus and in [dependence upon His person, giving praise to God the Father through Him.*

*   *   *

Years ago, my husband and I had business through which we became acquainted with a friend of Jesse Duplantis. Jesse's friend and my husband were on the phone together when Jesse called on another line to let his friend know he was already at his destination. Jesse had stopped by his friend's office on his way out of town.

The trip should have taken several hours, three, I think. Jesse made it in thirty minutes. He said he had raised his hands to praise God just before he merged onto the freeway. Suddenly, Jesse was at the destination—car and all.

God had an assignment for Jesse to pray for a very sick child. God needed him to be there at a specific time, so, He took care of the "transportation!" (Close Encounters of the God Kind by Jesse Duplantis.)

That incident was food for my spirit—a leap in faith and a revealing of possibilities! I had never imagined God worked like that on present day Earth! That was about three decades ago and God is still proving there is nothing impossible for Him. When heaven touches earth, expect the unexpected, believe the unbelievable, hear the unheard, and see the unseen. Experience the naturally supernatural life!

*   *   *

When I first began in full-time ministry, two friends and I met regularly at my home for prayer. It started out as a "normal" prayer meeting, but that didn't last long. We would start out in prayer—praying in the Spirit. We would find ourselves in strange places retrieving scrolls, treasures, talking with people of a different time or culture, or battling demonic forces. We were able to see each other and work together to accomplish the mission we didn't know we had.

One of my friends was given a spiritual coat (a mantle for warfare, if you would) that had various pockets filled with weapons none of us had ever seen or heard of. Sometimes she would pull out some sort of—item—wondering not only what it was but how to use it. Each time she was given the understanding and skill to operate the new weapon. Life in the Spirit is very interesting and the only predictable thing we found was that when Holy Spirit leads you in He will get you out, unharmed. Do not try to enter that realm on your own whim or out of curiosity. Yield to the Spirit of God. Be sure the Lord goes before you and always, always obey His direction. (See Foreword)

*   *   *

For years I had a world map on one of the walls of my office. Each night I would sit before that map and pray in the Spirit until I was given direction on what nation or state to pray for. I would pray thirty minutes to an hour, then go to bed. As soon as my head hit the pillow I would begin "seeing" crisis situations; accidents about to happen—wrecks in the making, someone stalking someone else with intent to commit murder, all manner of tragedy in the making. Each time I saw something like this I would leap into prayer in the Spirit. Because I actually experienced the urgency of each situation, I would react physically as if I were there. I might throw up my hands to stop an eighteen-wheeler about to crush a small car. Sometimes, I could feel my hands on a steering wheel or my feet slamming on the breaks to avoid a head-on collision. At other times, I was swerving to avoid something on the freeway. All the while, thinking I needed to get to sleep because I had to be at work in a few hours. Always, these were heart-pounding situations.

One night I asked the Lord why we didn't take care of this stuff while I was in my "prayer room." He told me I was His, "under-cover agent."

Occasionally, I would wonder if these things were happening somewhere, and was I really intervening or what was actually going on. (God is so faithful. All we have to do is ask. He doesn't withhold what we need, or sometimes, even just want to know.) So, in answer to "my wondering," the Lord revealed the reality of Kingdom work through spontaneous—crisis management—prayer. In other words, He used me in a situation that could be verified.

One of these "crisis management" prayers involved an older model red and white car. I don't remember the make or model, I think it was a '58 Chevy, but I'm not certain now. I watched as the car crossed over the Summit Avenue overpass and merge onto the West Freeway. (Having lived in Fort Worth for decades, I knew exactly where this was.) It was very cold and icy that night. The car spun out of control. There was other traffic in all three lanes and a high embankment on one side. Of course, Holy Spirit took over and prayer was activated, tongues flooding out of my mouth. I didn't see the end result; I had never seen the end result of my "work" as an "under-cover agent."

A few days later, I talked with one of the Advisors for the Weatherford Aglow Chapter of which I was President. It wasn't a scheduled meeting, I just had a few prayer points I needed to discuss, so, I stopped by his house. As we talked, he shared an experience he had had the previous week. He told me that his wife had been in the hospital in Fort Worth and he had driven there to visit her and stayed quite late. When he left the hospital, crossed over the Summit Avenue overpass and merged onto the freeway, his car spun out of control. He said it was miracle he didn't hit anyone nor were any other accidents caused as other drivers avoided him. Of course, that got my attention right away. I knew he drove a pick-up, but I had to ask:

"What kind of vehicle were you in?"

"I was driving my classic (whatever)."

Need I say, he had my full attention? I was very excited!

"What does it look like?! What color is it?!"

"Do you want to see it? Come outside. I'll show you."

There sat the car I had seen spin out on the West Freeway. Summit Avenue is the exit for the hospital district in that area of Fort Worth. This "under-cover work" really was doing exploits for God! After that I was eager to get to bed so I could "go to work." I still have these experiences, but not as often as during that time.

Exploits done in the Spirit
have a profound effect on earth.

*   *   *

Sometimes, I'm approached by people I don't know, but we know that we know each other. On most such occasions it's because we've met in the Spirit. One such incident occurred when I was attending an event celebrating "Bob" successfully passing his legal bar exam. He was now a "full fledged" attorney. As soon as I walked into my friend's house, I saw a man across the room with a look of surprised recognition on his face. I didn't recognize him so did not respond.

The man approached me and asked where he knew me from. I asked him what line of work he was in, perhaps we worked at the same place or were in some way work related. He told me he was a minister. I assumed we had met while "on assignment" in the spirit. However, the denomination of his ordination doesn't embrace such teachings, so I said nothing. Yet—he persisted in trying to discover how he knew me. He followed me around while I visited with our host and with other friends who were attending this event. When I left, the man followed me out to my car insisting we knew each other. So I said, "I pray for Bob."

This man said, "So do I. I'm his pastor."

I said, "Then, we've met in the Spirit while we were interceding for him."

The look on his face told me this was a totally new concept for him. I got in my car and drove off, seeing him in my review mirror, still standing in the street.

Reports abound of individuals who are approached by citizens from countries, which those sharing the experience have never visited. The people from the other countries testify, "You came to my country and led me to the Lord." (Or various other things.)

These type incidents happen when we stop trying to maintain "normality" and release control. If we yield to Holy Spirit and step into our natural habit—the Spirit realm, lives will be saved and salvations will spring forth.

Without the "me" factor, in doing exploits for God,
we become world changers!

* * *

Habitation is not something we strive after. It isn't a "sometime" thing. Habitation happens when we ask Jesus to be Lord of our lives. Holy Spirit moves right in. The thing is, we often don't recognize what has happened. We see that our attitudes are changing. We just don't realize it's because we're inhabited by the Spirit of the Living God. It isn't a matter of moving from visiting with God—Father, Son and/or Holy Spirit—to living with them. It's actually just recognizing they dwell in us! Yes, They!

Jesus said He would ask the Father who would send the Spirit of Truth (Holy Spirit) who will live with us constantly and would be in us. He further states that if we love Him and keep His command, He and the Father will make their special dwelling place in us [John 14:16-23]. Paul reiterates this:

For in Him the whole fullness of Deity (the Godhead) continues to dwell in bodily form [giving complete expression of the divine nature]. And you are in Him, made full and having come to fullness of life [in Christ you too are filled with the Godhead—Father, Son and Holy Spirit—and reach full spiritual stature]. And He is the Head of all rule and authority of every angelic principality and power] [Colossians 2:9-10].

Let your character or moral disposition be free from love of money [including greed, avarice, lust, and craving for earthly possessions] and be satisfied with your present [circumstances and with what you have]; for He [God] Himself has said, I will not in any way fail you nor give you up nor leave you without support. [I will] not, [I will] not, [I will] not in any degree leave you helpless nor forsake nor let [you] down (relax My hold on you)! [Assuredly not!] [Hebrews 13:5].

Jesus, Himself, assures us in Matthew:

Jesus approached and, breaking the silence, said to them, All authority (all power of rule) in heaven and on earth has been given to Me. Go then and make disciples of all the nations, baptizing them into the name of the Father and of the Son and of the Holy Spirit, teaching them to observe everything that I have commanded you, and behold, I am with you all the days (perpetually, uniformly, and on every occasion), to the very close and consummation of the age. Amen (so let it be) [Matthew 28:18-20].

We are not alone. We are the temple of Holy Spirit and a

special dwelling place for God the Father and God the Son. We, as Blood bought Christians, are already part of the Kingdom of God. Habitation is becoming aware that we are sons and daughters of Almighty God!

- Don't be concerned about protocol or titles, just be sure to be led by Holy Spirit.
- Holy Spirit will guide us.
- Practice being aware that we are walking, talking temples of Holy Spirit; a special dwelling for Jesus and Father God.
- Make decisions based upon knowledge of the ways and principles of God, cooperating with the leading of Holy Spirit.
- We need to consciously permit that knowledge to affect our manner of living.
- The more conscious we are of the indwelling God, the more we become changed to reflect His character and attributes.
- We will do what Jesus did, and greater works as well [John 14:12].
- We will do exploits for God.

* * * * * * * * *

EXERCISES

1. Surrender fully to being the Habitation you are and to the Triune God who dwells within.
2. Ask Holy Spirit to show you the renovations that have been made to the temple that is YOU.
3. Ask Holy Spirit to develop or increase the "Heart of the House"—a heart of worship.
4. Ask the Lord to give you a tour of the special dwelling place you are becoming.

5. Ask the Lord to show you the blueprints for renovations and expansion He has for you.

Psalm 45:1
My heart overflows with a goodly theme:
I address my psalm to a King. My tongue is like the pen of a
ready writer.

Matthew 28:18-20
Jesus approached and, breaking the silence, said to them,
All authority (all power of rule) in heaven and on earth has been
given to Me.
Go then and make disciples of all the nations,
baptizing them into the name of the Father and of the Son and of the
Holy Spirit,
Teaching them to observe everything that I have commanded you,
and behold,
I am with you all the days (perpetually, uniformly, and on every
occasion), to the [very] close and consummation of the age.
Amen (so let it be).

LEADING GROUPS
INTO
VISITATION

Doing Exploits For Our God

. . .the people who know their God shall prove themselves strong and shall stand firm and do exploits [for God]. And they who are wise and understanding among the people shall instruct many and make them understand. . . Daniel 11:32b-33a

Throughout time, God has revealed Himself—made Himself real to individuals and nations through dreams, visions and visitations. Yes, He reveals Himself to us through His Word. His desire is for us to desire relationship developing an intimacy that leads to continual communion. He wants to have a naturally supernatural relationship with us because that is our true nature. We are by nature, supernatural, because we are created in His likeness and image.

Communicating with and participating with the supernatural through the avenue of Holy Spirit is a safe and rewarding journey. If you are planning to lead a group into visitation, the first step is to be certain you are spiritually prepared. Paul said he wished everyone prayed in tongues. He also said he prayed in tongues more than anyone else. That's the way to approach leading visitation.

- You visit more than anyone else.
- Keep your line of communication with Holy Spirit open:
  - Pray in the Spirit—in tongues as Paul did.
  - Confess and repent of any known sin.
  - Ask the Lord to show you anything hidden, i.e., anything that would hinder communicating with Him or interrupt the flow of the anointing.
  - Keep short accounts with Him. We are told that if we confess our sins *He is faithful and just to forgive us our sins and forgive us of all unrighteousness* [1 John 1:9]. Confess and repent as soon as you are aware of a shortcoming.
  - Prepare the meeting place with worship music and prayer.
    - If it's your home, apply the Blood of the Lamb to your doors. (Some call this, "pleading" the Blood.)
      - I live in an apartment building so I not only anoint my door, but I also go down to the main entrance and anoint/apply the Blood there. I also anoint the bottom of the stairs and the elevator.
    - Declare no demonic force of any type or nature will be able to operate in that building.
    - Pronounce deafness to every demonic force or entity that is sent to listen and blindness to every ungodly watcher.

- Loose the angels to guard and minister according to their assignment.
- Anoint everyone at the door.
  - I anoint people in the hallway before they enter my apartment.
  - The Lord often gives brief prophetic declarations for individuals.

Public Venue:

- If it's a public venue, arrive an hour early so you can cleanse and set the atmosphere of the room.
  - If you can't get into the room early, walk around the area or even sit in your car praying and making declarations over the meeting. These things don't require the "natural touch" although prophetic acts are very powerful.
  - Continue as you would for your home.

Time:

I normally limit group meetings to two hours. That gives time for teaching, entering in, and for everyone to briefly share their experience. To help you get started, I have included examples of a few brief teachings I have given. These are simply examples and do not follow a particular pattern. They not intended to structure your meetings. The most important thing is to follow the leading of Holy Spirit. He may have prepared hearts for a particular impartation that doesn't fit the teaching you expect to deliver. Follow His lead. He won't disappoint you.

I have found that soft instrumental music is very helpful during meetings. Some leaders I know prefer using vocals. Again, each meeting, follow the leading of Holy Spirit.

Don't be alarmed if some members of the group see demons and/or inappropriate things. This is a barometer of the need for housecleaning in their soul. Encourage people to not be ashamed if this occurs. Confessing/sharing such experiences bring them into the light of truth which is the avenue for deliverance. Teach them to rebuke the enemy and to refuse any of his offerings. Most of the time people are willing to press in and gain freedom by entering into visitation with their hearts and mind "stayed," fixed on the Lord.

If you are anointed for deliverance ministry and have time following the meeting, invite them to stay for a brief time of personal ministry. Ask others to stay and assist. If you can't minister following the meeting, schedule a time they can return for personal ministry. If you are not assigned to deliverance ministry, put them in contact with someone who is.

The enemy will attempt to use every venue available to disrupt what the Lord wants to do during these meetings, including—or perhaps, especially your soft heart or your proclivity to certain issues. Keep focused on the purpose of the meeting.

I suggest everyone write their visitations and review them at least once. So much happens in that realm our consciousness is not able to capture everything. When we review our experience, often the Lord reveals much more to us. When He "reminds" us, our spirit bears witness and prompts our consciousness to remembrance.

If we don't purpose ourselves to gain the complete understanding, we can miss important revelation intended to be building blocks for our future. At times we are given warfare strategies for our own lives as well as for our community, state and/or nation. In the "remembering" is often when we discover the key to our next step.

At the end of the visitation, encourage everyone to share

their experience. Three to five minutes is normally enough time per person. This often leads to completion of what began in the Spirit and can increase our understanding. Sharing also helps anchor the memory of the experience.

If individuals in your group have been deeply wounded it is often very difficult for them to accept, let alone interpret the loving kindness experienced in the manifest presence of the Lord. I was one of those. My inner man (soul) and my inmost man (my spirit) were wrapped so tightly in the blanket of woundedness I could not receive His love. I certainly couldn't return it. All of the ministry I received from well-meaning, caring friends and ministers made very small, short inroads past my "no trespassing" boundary. BUT, JESUS, HOLY SPIRIT, and FATHER GOD, shattered my fortress and built me a new home in Them! Their method was face-to-face experiences, some of which are vignetted in this book. That was nearly two decades ago. The Lord has continued my renovation, taking it to the next level, often through the experiences of those who attend my home meetings.

If you have seasoned, spiritual warriors in your group, there may be times the visitations include acts of war against our enemy—satan and his minions. This can be a very good thing. However, if warfare becomes the focus of your group, the wounded and those very young in the spirit—new to the concept of face to face relationship with the Lord, may abandon their hope for spiritual advancement. More likely than not, they will leave the group. If you are called to warfare and have two or more people with this anointing in your group, talk to them about forming a separate group with the focus on warfare. Groups do not have to be large to be effective in the Spirit.

Designating a focus brings the group together in one accord. The Sea of Galilee, the throne room, the Garden of Eden, or the well of His presence are examples of focus, even a path through the woods. The anointing is always strengthened when people are of one mind. However, because everyone is in different stages of development, be sure to let them know that while you are "leading," if the Lord appears to them and draws them away they are to follow Him. The meetings really are not about getting the lesson across as much as they are to set the atmosphere for the group to enter into the presence of the Lord. Your job in this ministry is very much like that of a Butler. Through teaching revelation, you open the doors and windows so others can see and enter in.

Prepare as He directs. Although the Lord will minister to you while others are "caught up" or captivated in His presence, I suggest you remain alert to those in the group, being available if there are questions or if someone is having difficulty entering in. If a person or persons do have difficulty entering in, I suggest taking them to another room so their questions and your instructions do not disturb those who are already in His manifest presence.

Encourage the group to purposely enter into visitation daily. The ultimate goal of teaching "visitation" is for people to move into the understanding and awareness of habitation. Practicing our senses is the route to awareness [Hebrews 5:14]

The following 'teachings' are merely examples. Let Holy Spirit set each meeting, He'll focus on the needs of those attending.

Refrain from inventing or making up an experience for the group. Be led/instructed by Holy Spirit.

* TEACHING *

THE SPIRIT OF RELIGION

Exodus 33:18-23
John 20:24-29

Some people have a difficult time "seeing" God—Father, Son, or Holy Spirit—because they have been taught:
- No man can see God and live (This is scriptural).
- It is more blessed to believe without seeing (This, also, is scriptural.)

Let's look a little more closely at this:

Every Scripture is God-breathed (given by His inspiration) and profitable for instruction, for reproof and conviction of sin, for correction of error and discipline in obedience, [and] for training in righteousness (in holy living, in conformity to God's will in thought, purpose, and action), 2 Timothy 3:16.

- Do we still have to make blood sacrifices to cover sin?
  - NO! Since the Cross of Christ, no other blood sacrifice is acceptable:
    - Psalm 50:7-15
    - Hebrews 9 (especially verses 11-14)
    - Hebrews 10:1-6

With this in mind, let's look at Exodus 33:18-23 from this side of the cross. Because of the death, burial and resurrection of Jesus Christ, what we refer to as salvation turns us as individuals into a dwelling place for Him. He is in us and we are in Him.

- Didn't Jesus say when we see Him we see the Father ?

- When the "Him" in us looks into the face of the Father, are we not looking as well?
- Does He cover the eyes of our spirit man with His hand so when He looks at Father we won't see?
- When we are invited to go boldly before the throne of grace are we to be blindfolded first? No.
- Are we not to see what He sees, hear what He hears, do what He did and even greater things because He went to the Father? Now, they all make their special dwelling place in us!
  o This should be an even closer relationship than we have with our parents or our spouses. They don't live in us.

Let's take another look at John 20:24-29. Yes, Jesus does say, *Because you have seen Me, Thomas, do you now believe (trust, have faith)? Blessed and happy and to be envied are those who have never seen Me and yet have believed and adhered to and trusted and relied on Me.*

After this experience, Thomas continued seeing Jesus. He didn't forbid himself to look into the eyes of Jesus because he had once doubted. He spent time with Jesus every chance he got, up to and including the ascension.

Guess what! We, most of us, if not all, have first believed without seeing. Like Job, we *have heard with the hearing of our ears.* So, anyone who is hung up on needing to believe without seeing, you have already passed that test.

Now, it's time to get to know and trust the one in whom you have believed. Trust Him to show you the unseen. Be willing to hear the unheard. Trust Him to heal you in ways you didn't know you needed healing. Trust Him to give you revelation and understanding of the mysteries of God. Trust Him to use you in ways you've never heard of anyone being used before. TRUST HIM!

Some may be hindered because they feel unworthy. This can be from a feeling of guilt or due to the spirit of religion. Anyone who has accepted Jesus as Lord and Savior is qualified and made worthy by and through His Blood. He loves each of us and gave Himself for us—He won't turn us away when we seek His face. Give yourself permission to SEE and experience the presence of the triune God!

He chooses to make Himself real to us [John 14:20-23]. His desire is that we can be where He is [John 14:3]. Selah—pause and think on the implications of that!

"In the name and authority of Jesus Christ, whose I am and whom I serve, and by the power of the blood and the Spirit of God, I bind the spirit of religion and loose my precious friends to hear, see, understand, and move as Holy Spirit directs."

APPLICATION

- Pause. Give yourself time to receive direction from Holy Spirit. Ask the Lord to send angels to escort the members to the Throne Room
- Narrate what you are seeing until you perceive they are captivated by the Spirit of God.
    - If you are not seeing anything, silence is an awesome vehicle for the presence of God to fill.

* TEACHING *

BUILDING INTIMACY WITH THE LORD

The Well of His Presence

Psalm 105:1-5

*O Give thanks unto the Lord, call upon His name, make known His
doings among the peoples
Sing to Him, sing praises to Him; meditate on and talk of all His
marvelous deeds and devoutly praise them.
Glory in His holy name: let the hearts of those rejoice who seek
and require the Lord as their indispensable necessity.
Seek. Inquire of and for the Lord and crave Him and His strength
(His might and inflexibility to temptation):
Seek and require His face and His presence continually evermore.
Earnestly remember the marvelous deeds that He has done. His
miracles and wonders, the judgments and sentences which He
pronounced upon His enemies as in Egypt.*

Psalm 139:7-14

*Where could I go from Your Spirit? Or where could I flee from
Your presence?
If I ascend up into heaven, You are there;
if I make my bed in Sheol (the place of the dead), behold, You are
there.
If I take the wings of the morning or dwell in the uttermost parts of
the sea,
Even there shall Your hand lead me, and Your right hand shall
hold me.
If I say, Surely the darkness shall cover me and the night shall be
[the only] light about me,
Even the darkness hides nothing from You, but the night shines as*

the day; the darkness and the light are both alike to You.
For You did form my inward parts; You did knit me together in my mother's womb.
I will confess and praise You for You are fearful and wonderful and for the awful wonder of my birth! Wonderful are Your works, and that my inner self knows right well.

Teaching through these two portions of Psalms will help everyone understand God's great love for us.

It isn't necessary to have a "prophetic gift" or a "seer anointing" or even the gift of faith to experience visitation with the Lord. It only requires desire for relationship. If you have a desire for deeper, more intimate relationship with the Lord, you have enough faith to believe it is possible.

APPLICATION

- Remind the group of the time Jesus met the Samaritan woman at the well.
  - Though she was an idol worshipper, an adulteress, deceptive and arrogant—still—Jesus wanted a personal relationship with her.
- Narrate what you see as you are entering into the time of visitation.

* TEACHING *

AND A BOOK WAS WRITTEN

Scriptures tell of numerous books, many written here on earth—some ordered to be written by kings—others by prophets; a number of others written in heaven.

- We all know about the Lamb's Book of Life [Philippians 4:3 and Revelation-numerous scriptures].

- But, there are also books written on each of us, recording our substance even before we were born [Psalm 139:16].

- There is a book of deeds and works—our way of feeling and acting; our aims and endeavors [Revelation 20:12].

- There is even a book of remembrance wherein is recorded every instance when we think on His name or talk with others about Him [Malachi 3:17].

- If we have accepted the sacrifice of the Lamb of God and have overcome, our names are written in the Book of Life [Philippians 4:3, Revelation 3:5, 20:12, 21:27].

- When you search the scriptures, you'll find numerous references to books, such as how important our tears are to God—our tears are caught in a bottle and written a book [Psalm 56:8].

- If someone isn't sure some wrong they committed has been removed [Psalm 103:12], even though they have repeatedly repented—they may find the incident has been erased from the Book of Deeds and Works [Revelation 20:12].

- Perhaps someone is still waiting for the fulfillment of a promise.
  - They may be able to find encouragement in one of the books written in heaven [Romans 11:29, 2 Corinthians 1:20, Hebrews 6:12].

APPLICATION

Narrate what you are experiencing. This is not to be an excursion for intellectual enrichment. Rather it is a tool to gain a deeper understanding of how important each person is to the Lord and how great a love He has for us.

* TEACHING *

GOD'S GIFTS AND CALLING ARE IRREVOCABLE

Romans 11:29

Recently, while ministering at a church, I saw the people as pomegranates full of seeds of promise, gifts, and callings. I knew the members were faithful and wanted the congregation to grow. Each person there has seeds to sow into the call of the church and into their own dreams. Often our gifts to our church body are equated with our tithes and offerings. There's more—so much more.

As I studied, I discovered that gifts are related to forgiveness. Gift, the Greek word charisma, does mean a freely given gift and can refer to natural or spiritual gifts including faith, holiness, virtue, etc. The immediate root word, chrizomai, is used 23 times in the Bible. Eleven of those 23 times it is translated 'forgive'. One time it is translated, 'frankly forgive'. For our spiritual gifts to be activated and operate properly, we must be forgiven—and—we must forgive as we have been freely and frankly forgiven.

Calling means to receive an invitation or a new name. The Jews have a custom whereby they are given a new name to mark certain advancements, progress in their lives. We see this in the Catholic church as well; Judy may become Sister Mary Catherine. A man named Peter may become Father Benedict. We see this in marriage customs—a woman often lays aside her maiden name and takes the last name of her husband. In some cultures, the husband's last name is simply added to the wife's maiden name, and children often receive both their father's name and their mother's maiden name. You see name or title change in the corporate world as well. An Executive Assistant may become

Supervisor. A President may become the Chief Executive Officer, and so on. In the military a "private" can work his way through the ranks with various name changes. It is often easier to for us and others to embrace our "new" station in life if our name is changed to reflect God's Purpose. This is a godly principle for which Abraham, Sarah, Jacob, Esther, Peter, and Paul are examples.

Often we don't fulfill our call because we don't understand the longing in our heart and the talents and skills we have are gifts from God for Kingdom building. We may not feel qualified. We may think it's too late for the desire of our heart to be fulfilled. He put that desire in us—called us for His purposes. If we only yield to Him, He will bring His plan to fruition.

> *For God's gifts and His call are irrevocable. He never withdraws them when once they are given and He does not change His mind about those to whom He gives His grace or to whom He sends His call* Romans 11:29.

That scripture is quite clear. We don't have to be kings and queens. We don't need a degree from a university (though it can be helpful at times). We don't have to be approved by a committee to flow in the gifts He has given and/or fulfill His appointment—call. However, keep this in mind—a person who is not submitted to and associated with others becomes an open target for demonic influence. Independence soon turns into rebellion, then what started out as an effort to fulfill our call results in failure and breeds woundedness, anger, and isolation.

If we are assigned to, or want to participate in, a particular organization or denomination, we do need to adhere to their rules and meet their qualifications as long as they don't go against the principles of God. Even though Paul was assigned to the nations and many of the Jewish cultural restrictions did not apply, Paul still submitted his teachings and beliefs to the council at Jerusalem and submitted to them. Don't rebel against the authority structure the Lord sets you under. Submission is a very important part of fulfilling your call.

Remember, when God sent angels to announce the birth of His Son, He sent them to shepherds. He notified foreigners by an unusual, never-before-seen star. And! He sent his son through a young girl who was engaged to a carpenter. Approximately two years later the king still didn't know nor did the priests, the teachers, the lawyers or the historians. He used and informed common, ordinary people.

God used people whom He had purposed for that specific time and who had specific, gifts and callings; not necessarily noble callings or highly desirable gifts. But, they were chosen people who said, "Yes," to their call.

Today, if we say, "Yes," what will God do through us?

Will we see His "call" as something less than what we want out of life? Or, perhaps, beyond our expectations for lives?

Will we see our "gift" as ordinary? Maybe, embarrassing? Or, perhaps, too lofty for our station in life?

APPLICATION

Though we often think we know what gifts we have, there may be gifts we are unaware of or don't understand. As you enter into visitation suggest each individual ask the Lord the following questions:

- Ask the Lord to reveal to you the gifts He has placed in you.

- Ask Him to show you unused gifts you may have not recognized or have not considered their value to Kingdom purposes.
- Ask Him to show you what calling He purposed you for.
- Ask Him if you're submitted properly.
- Whatever He shows you—yield to His plans and purposes.

Once we say, "Yes," He'll take care of the when and how.

* TEACHING *

THE LORD'S JEWELS

Malachi 3:15-16

Then those who feared the Lord talked often one to another:
and the Lord listened and heard it,
and a book of remembrance was written before Him of those who
reverenced and worshipfully feared the Lord and who thought on
His name.
And They shall be Mine, says the Lord of hosts,
in that day when I publicly recognize and
openly declare them to be My Jewels
(My special possession, My peculiar treasure).
And I will spare them, as a man spares his own son who serves
him.

We see in the above scripture that there are a certain type of people the Lord will treat in a special way—He will make them His jewels, special possession, His peculiar treasure. Qualifying characteristics to become a jewel include:

- Fear of the Lord.
- Talking often to one another about Him.
- Thinking on His name.

The word translated fear in this instance, actually does mean fear, to be afraid. A secondary meaning is to stand in awe of, be awed. Further amplification of the word fear is to reverence, honor and/or respect.

Some people magnify the "fear" part of this word. They tremble when they think of getting God's attention. Their emotional response is based upon a fear of His anger, so they withhold themselves from Him. The Children of Israel are an example of God's reaction to that. He basically said to Moses,

"Because they drew away from Me in fear, don't even let them set foot on this mountain." (paraphrased)

Now, I feared disobeying my parents because I didn't want to get a "whipping". But, I was not in fear of them—I wanted and received their hugs, their approval, their instruction. A healthy fear and being afraid are two different things. You see, when we are afraid, we miss out on all the good stuff and our character develops in an incomplete manner. We don't know how to receive love. We don't know how to give respect. We haven't a clue how to honor people. We develop contempt toward them. We dishonor them. We walk around feeling rejected and blame them for it.

Some people throw out the "fear" part of this word. As they develop, they are often over confident, sometimes obnoxious in their attitude toward others. Those in this group, also, do not know how to respect or honor others. They normally don't know how to love anyone more than they love themselves. In arrogance, they may even say, "I can do anything I want to because Daddy loves me!" Ooops!

I knew a woman who, had this attitude, though she was Spirit filled and in ministry. We went to a conference in New Orleans and she took that attitude into the French Quarter. We were not in the first business establishment more than five or ten minutes before she developed a severe headache. Her headache was so intense she couldn't walk by herself. I helped her out to a park bench near the river. Long story short, she became blind. When I got her back to the hotel she asked why this had happened to her but not me. I told her it was because she went in arrogance and pride. Of course, she denied that, but her attitude was obvious. The blindness lasted a few hours. Later, it became obvious that a spirit had entered her that birthed enmity between us. She became obsessed with destroying my ministry standing in the community. She told me she was the stick that would break my back.

We need to embrace the fullness of the meaning of the Hebrew word, fear. We need to learn to walk in righteousness, peace, and joy. Love needs to be our badge and discernment our strategy. We need to discern not only the intents of others; we need to discern and understand our own intentions and the root of our attitudes.

Now, let's look at the word, "make"—He will, "*make them His jewels.*" At first glance I thought this meant 'make' as in a collection. NOOOO! Here are a few of the possible definitions of the word translated 'make':

- Fashion
- Act with effect
- Prepare
- To make or give an offering
- Attend or put in order
- To appoint, ordain, institute
- To spend, be used
- To press or squeeze

There is a process to the making of jewels. Pearls begin as an irritating intrusion in the shell of a clam. The clam secrets a substance that coats the irritant layer after layer until it is removed by man who names it 'pearl'. Opals are formed by a long, repeated process of water washing silicon dioxide particles from sandstone into cracks and crevices, layering and re-layering until the opalescence forms. Geologists still don't know exactly how rubies are formed. They understand the components required to form the beauty of the red jewel, but have yet to decipher the exact process. Rubies are still one of God's special mysteries.

Though coal placed under the right conditions can be the birthplace diamonds, most often their development is the result of a catastrophic event that goes beyond the natural process of coal.

More often diamonds are "caught" in veins of coal. Diamond formation requires extreme pressure and heat such as when asteroids or meteorites hit earth or during volcanic eruptions. The natural birthing place for diamonds is ninety miles below the earth's surface. The movement of Earth's mantle and subterranean plates push the diamonds toward the surface and they are deposited in coal veins on their journey. (Information on gem formation acquired from geology. com)

After centuries of development, the 'raw' stones require a lot of work to become beautiful. A jeweler polishes and cuts until the beauty is evident to every eye.

Our Jeweler disciplines or corrects those He loves Proverbs 3:12. His methods of correction and/or discipline are not always easy or comfortable to us, but they are always effective. Our reaction to His methods are very important. A spot in a diamond devalues it. A spot in one of His jewels is simply an opportunity for Him to display His great love as He polishes and shapes us which increases our value in the Kingdom of God when He presents us without spot or wrinkle Ephesians 5:25-27.

When the Lord points out a spot in our character or attitude—we shouldn't be afraid or ashamed. He's making us into a jewel for His treasury. The pressing, squeezing, layering, washing and polishing may not be fun, but it will be profitable.

APPLICATION

- Ask the Lord to take the group to His treasure house.
- Ask that their eyes be opened to see the various jewels.
- Ask that they be able to see the peculiar treasure they are.
- Ask that they be affirmed.
- Ask that, if there is a spot or wrinkle He wants to deal with, it be exposed to them and they yield to His loving discipline.

4/2007
Commissioning

"This one has been wrested from the hand of our enemy. She has suffered much by his hand, but she has overcome. She has become strong as the web of a spider and cunning as a serpent. She has learned how to wield the Sword by the hand yielded to My Spirit. She has learned the power of compassion and the softness of fire. She has warred and she has hidden in caves. She has been wounded and has insisted on healing—not giving place to bitterness, pride or anger. She is Mine and is ready for commissioning."

I fall on my face, but without touching me or even moving, the Great God lifts me to a standing position with the force of His eyes. I see as it were white scales on my own eyes. They have the effect of sunglasses and I know they are to protect my eyes from the blinding glory of The Most High God. I am able to see those who stand by the throne. They are tall and slender, seemingly at attention but with their hands behind their back. They don't actually look like angels yet I know they are. (My Lord sends thoughts to me: *"They are messengers—ready to take the Words of Our Father as He directs.)*

As the voice of God rumbles, vibrating through my being, words of affirmation fill the air. I see demons struck with terror. I see angels honoring me with their eyes, wondering at the mystery they are seeing unfold. As the Father continues speaking, the demons become more terrified and I see their princes come to see what's going on. They, too, become terrified. Satan pulls his hair and roars.

A VISITATION SAMPLER

The following pages contain experiences from various individuals for whom I have been honored to be the vessel the Lord has used to open the doors of possibility. Their experiences are presented here with their permission in their own words.

⚓ ⚓ ⚓

CAROL D.
3/18/2013
Soul Wounds

I walked into a beautiful garden and saw a large tree in the distance. It wasn't very tall but was really broad and full. It seemed to draw me to it, but as I got closer I noticed something strange about it. Half of it was healthy with bright shiny green leaves and huge shiny red apples. The other half had dull, dark green leaves and the fruit was shriveled and wormy.

Suddenly, a bolt of lightning struck the tree and it split down the middle. The unhealthy half fell over, blackened. When it hit the ground I felt the shock of it. The ground around the tree turned gray and the grayness slowly spread outward turning everything it touched gray. As it started coming towards me I tried to move to get away from it but I seemed frozen to the spot. My eyes and throat were badly stinging from the acrid stench. I kept trying to get free as it moved nearer and nearer. Suddenly, I was gray also, but now I could move.

I walked to the side of the tree that was healthy and saw a clear blue stream meandering along a short distance from me. I went over to it to try to wash my eyes out to stop the stinging but it didn't help, so I just sat down on the bank and put my feet in the water.

I saw someone out of the corner of my eye walking towards me. I looked over and saw Jesus coming. He had on a long sleeved white shirt and white pants. His pants were rolled up to the knee. He came over and sat down beside me and put his feet in the water. He reached over and held my hand. That was the end of my visitation for that night.

The next morning during my devotions, I asked Jesus to come talk with me again as I had several questions from the night before.

Jesus told me that it wasn't a bolt of lightning that had struck the tree; it was His Glory Light, severing old from new. I asked Him why everything had turned gray and why I was still gray even after He had held my hand.

He said it was ashes from the tree disintegrating that had covered everything.

I asked why I had been unable to move until I had gotten covered with the ashes too. He told me to read Jeremiah 31:40. This verse says:

"And the whole valley of the dead bodies and of the ashes and all the fields as far as the brook Kidron, to the

corner of the horse gate, toward the east shall be holy to the Lord. It will not be plucked up or overthrown anymore, forever."

He said I needed to be covered by the ashes of my past, therefore to be holy, never to be cloaked again. I asked Him what He meant by "cloaked." He showed me myself and I was covered head to toe with a gray, hooded cloak, like a second skin. It was not flowing and was zipped from the hem up to my neck where it was fastened with a padlock.

I asked Him how to get it off and He said, "As My Glory Light severed the old from the new, the good from the bad when it split the tree in half, My light has severed all ungodly soul ties in you. It has healed and sealed all soul wounds."

I asked why I still felt greatly disturbed, sad, weighted down. He said, "It's familiar." Then He was gone.

I started trying to figure out what He had meant by "familiar" when it clicked. "Familiar," was the cloak I was wearing. It was feelings, ideas, expectations, etc., I had lived with all of my life that were the result of all the soul wounds and ungodly soul ties.

I stood up and started declaring and decreeing that I was free; free of all past encumbrances, all ties. I told the demons in me, on me, and around me that they had lost all legal rights and that after they cleaned up any messes and damages they had made in me, they had to go straight into the Abyss and could never come bother me again.

I still felt the weight of the "cloak" but knew it would be gone soon.

❧ ❧ ❧

SHERRY B.
2013
Jesus and Me on the Chrystal Sea

It is the most beautiful place to be.
I find Him waiting there always for me.

When I come to the place of His embrace
He makes me feel so lovely as I look into His face.

There is no place I would rather be than with Jesus on the Crystal
Sea.
Once, I couldn't go there. Was it sin or shame, guilt or pain?
Had I lost my place on the Crystal Sea?
I took my sin, shame, guilt and pain,
I left them with my Savior on the Crystal Sea.

It was not He was disappointed in me.
It was me who was disappointed in me.

How wonderful it is to know that I can meet with Jesus on the
Crystal Sea.
He always touches my heart and heals me.

Now I wear an ermine robe as I meet my Savior King on the
Crystal Sea.
He is so lovely and beautiful to me as I dance with my Groom
whose bride I will be.

I could go on forever with the wonderful things He has for me.
As I dance with Jesus on the Crystal Sea.

— — —

LOIS B.
4/10/2013
– Appearance –
Holy Ghost
Or
Jesus?

On Wednesday evening, April 10, 2013, shortly after six or six thirty, I was attempting to sing along with the worship leaders in our mid-week meeting. My eyes were drawn to the wall behind the singers where a large cross hangs. A stillness I cannot describe came over me. I could not move or avert my eyes away from the cross on the wall behind the singers. It almost reaches the ceiling. It has a purple drape hung over the "tee" part of the cross and a crown of thorns adorning the cross-section. It is auspicious in itself.

Why, I do not know, or did not know, there appeared on the dark yellow wall where the cross hangs, a lighter color around the cross in the shape of a cloaked . . . BEING, . . . head and all (as was worn in the days of Jesus) with outstretched arms.

My subconscious mind, after realizing it wasn't going away and I could not tear my eyes away from the lighter area around the cross, I asked:

"Is that you, Jesus?"

No answer.

I was mesmerized by the aberration (being) on the wall. I thought I would explode from the pressure of wonder that I would be privileged to see this. Again, I asked, "Is that you, Jesus?" Tears filled my eyes and ran down my cheeks as I stared at the figure on the wall behind the cross. I think my heart knew the answer. I shifted my eyes to see if it disappeared, or if somehow the lighting made the area immediately around the cross lighter by far than the wall behind the cross. Surely it was some kind of shadow, or the lights were hanging in such a way to cause this. However, the figure stayed in my vision. I was distanced from the singing, as strong as it was. The music and the singers were as if in another place. My ears were almost muffled. I was transfixed on the sighting. I could not move. My mind was asking, again, "Is that You, Jesus? Are you telling me something? Am I going home to be with you tonight? Or maybe tomorrow, . . or when I take the tests at the hospital? I'm ready. Oh, Jesus, I'm ready. Is it time?"

No answer.

I blinked my eyes, squeezed them shut and shook my head, but the sighting did not leave. I averted my thoughts by wiping the tears streaming down my cheeks with a tissue from a box on the floor. This, I thought to be embarrassing from a fleshly point of view. I thought to myself, *I'm going crazy or—my imagination is running away.* Still the figure was there.

I don't know how much time passed, or how long this lasted, but when the singing ended, Pastor stood to say something and I heard him announce an offering would be taken, I hesitated momentarily to leave Jesus (as I saw the figure to be), but finally forced my eyes off the wall to do what I needed to do. I always contributed; it would be out of place if I didn't. I opened my billfold and contributed to the evening's offering. That done, I looked again to the wall, but the sighting was gone. The wall was dark yellow again. *Oh, Dear God, Jesus, where did you go? I am going crazy.*

Oh, no, Jesus don't leave! I silently cried. *We need you.*

No answer—no figure any longer. My heart crashed. Had anyone noticed my condition? I hoped not as it would seem irrational. This was not a vision, I knew it was not a vision as I had experienced one some time ago and know what a visitation is. This was a phenomenal happening, one I shall never forget and am ever grateful for. All the praying I did, asking God to reveal Himself to me was now surely happening. I need to verify this with two others.

A peace I have not known for a long time came over me after I left the church, and I no longer feared the next two days of tests at the hospital. Added to that, I no longer fear being lonely.

Praise the Lord, O my soul, Praise the Lord.

Now, I asked God, should I share this or is it just for me? The answer I found in the Holy Word, is:

Write these things for others to see.

Am I doing the right thing? Would anyone understand, or is this my imagination again?

No.

I'm to do God's will, as tears fill my eyes.

❧ ❧ ❧

PENNY H.
2013
Reconciliation

In this visitation, Velma instructed us to fly up a mountain. Amazingly enough I flew right up to the top like I was an expert. I flew like Wendy in Peter Pan, but without the pixie dust. It must have been four or five thousand feet up, because of all the green lush vegetation growing up the side. A white tent was pitched with the flaps opened invitingly. The tent was to represent Holy Spirit.

I landed in front of the opening and was drawn in. The decor was warm and inviting. Tapestries were hanging on the walls, rugs and pillows carpeted the floor. A couch was scooted up against one wall of the tent. On the opposite side across from the couch the floor was piled high with plush colorful pillows to sit on.

Before the visitation began Velma was sharing and teaching. I smelled cherry tobacco. This smell was just like the kind my father smoked in his pipe.

The atmosphere was peaceful and cozy upon entering. I was feeling very at home and relaxed on the cushions on the floor. Peace was tangible, I felt like I was able to breathe it, when Jesus came strolling in playing a harp. He sat on the couch across from me softly playing. Enjoying listening to the music, I again smelled the cherry tobacco.

I noticed a movement out of the corner of my eye in my peripheral vision, I turned toward the opening. As I did my father who has been dead for fifteen years came through the tent flaps. Shocked I said, "Daddy!" He came and kneeled in front of me and said, "Penny, please forgive me for hurting and wounding you. I love you very much." He then hugged me and I thought *"This is the first time he has ever hugged me."*

I got the impression he wanted to go outside, I didn't want to leave Jesus. Jesus said it was okay, He would still be here when I got back. So, I went for a walk with my dad.

He held my hand as we strolled in the mountain pasture, this was a first, too. My dad reaffirmed his love for me then he disappeared like smoke rising in the wind.

I shot up like a rocket, filled with joy and flew as high as I could. Then like a jet, I bent over backwards and free falling all the way down to a river, I continued to drop down till just inches from impact. I then leveled off and glided along the surface of the water soaring back up to where Jesus was waiting for me. He was still playing the Harp as I entered the tent.

It was so wonderful to be in the presence of my Lord and to see my father again. Years of hurts and misunder-standings were healed in a moment's time.

ᴏ— ᴏ— ᴏ—

FRAN S.
2006
First Visitation

While on a telephone visit with a friend, she said something about my secret place with the Father. That would be a good place to be, especially if I kept finding myself without sleep which was robbing my rest. I just wasn't aware of the scripture and instances in the Bible of various ways to visit with The Father. She said surely there was somewhere you loved to go as a young girl to be by yourself.

Well, there was! After getting cleaned up in my fresh 'flour sack' dress mother had made, she would let me visit the neighbor girl. Sometimes she couldn't come out just then, and her mother would give me a peanut butter and jelly sandwich folded over and I would go behind their house in a small clearing where there was this huge rock, climb upon it and eat my wonderful sandwich.

So one night, sleep wouldn't come. I pictured myself on this rock, a little girl with her sandwich. I just watched her. She loved being there. So peaceful and refreshing. Not a care in the world. While observing her, the rock changed. Right under where she was sitting, the rock began to jut out as if a drawer was there and being pulled out. It made a ledge. I was fascinated! While still

143

wondering at the change, the rock made another change. Right below the new ledge another ledge jutted out underneath that first one and farther out. I NOW HAD A THREE LAYER ROCK. Well, as I said, it was so peaceful there. When I finally looked up from the changing of the rock formation, as it didn't appear there was any more movement coming, there was this most wonderful river flowing straight in front of me and wound around out of my sight. It was most delightful to observe. Even now typing this and seeing it like I do so often, now I notice the River originates a great distance but straight down under me and the three layer rock. THEN I WOKE UP! IT WAS THE NEXT MORNING.

As time passed, many times I went to my THREE LAYER ROCK, which He revealed to me some time later was THE FATHER, SON AND THE HOLY SPIRIT.

The River—the River of Life! From this wonderful vantage point, He would then sometimes begin to show me other places and their meanings to me and to His plan for me. Later I read a book entitled The Secret Place. My, it's good. However for me, I was glad I hadn't read it so I knew of a certainty my original visit with The Three was from Him to me.

᠆ ᠆ ᠆

SANDRA M.
2013
Word of Life

Last night before I fell asleep I went on a journey. I saw myself dancing with Jesus in the atmosphere, very sweet time.

Then two angels came and escorted me up into the 3rd heaven. We were all laughing along the way and when we arrived in the 3rd heaven, we all were just rolling on the 'ground' with laughter. I noticed a rose bush next to me and the area under it was filled with gold dust and red jewels (instead of your typical bark)!

Then I was taken into the throne room and I melted on the floor before the Lord. I just soaked for a bit until He took me into another room that was separated from the throne room by these incredibly, beautiful silk curtains that felt so "delicious!"

I then fell asleep.

This morning I wanted to pick up where we left off...so I asked the Lord if we could do that. He led me again through the silk curtains—and I looked over and saw my two angels giggling at me. I looked at Jesus and He just was grinning also. He took me to a treasure chest and opened it up. He took out a beautiful leather-bound book and handed it to me. He told me this was the Word of Life for me.

I clutched it to my chest and it became immersed into me. The Lord told me that it was my very own personal manual for my life—my guide book. It is full of every situation and circumstance that I am yet to encounter. All that I need for wisdom, understanding, and revelation is in this guide book. When I am in a situation and feel confused or baffled - I just need to be reminded that God has given me all that I need—and I just need to refer to it.

As I'm writing this now I am aware that God has truly given us everything we need for life and godliness (2 Peter 1:3) ... and this is just how He makes it real and tangible to me!

Such a wonderful God He is!!!

o— o— o—

DIANA M.
2006
First Visitation
My path had rocks and gravel and the well was round with brick. The ladle of water, when I drank it at first, felt like a thud

when it hit my stomach the first time and then as I sipped the water it began to feel light and free. Then Jesus was there by a bluff above a stream of water and a waterfall. He hugged me and I feel so loved and giddy like a little girl. He told me there would be more laughter in my life and my heart feels so free and weightless.

"Jesus, why has it taken me so long to go through this healing?" I asked.

Jesus said, "Because you believe consciously but have some old teachings in your subconscious that are hindering the complete manifestation of your healing."

I ask, "Lord, when they talk about letting you be our husband when our earthly husbands aren't there for us, I don't understand."

Jesus said, "You are to totally trust Me to make you feel loved and safe and not to be bitter with your husband like My Word has told you to do."

"But God," I say, "It hurts and I feel so alone."

Jesus says, "That is because you are not letting Me hold you. You want to be so tough and get through it on your own. You need to reach out and take My hand and then You will feel love surround you and all hurt and loneliness will leave and then you will have a better attitude and presence around you and others will sense this in you."

All of a sudden, yellow roses start popping up everywhere and I am so excited because I love yellow roses and Jesus said, "See? Here are your yellow roses you love so much. Drink in their smell and along with that you are drinking in My love for you and My peace."

Now Jesus and I sit and smell the roses and listen to the

waterfall and I feel so secure and peaceful and safe.

Jesus says, "Remember, 'No weapon formed against you will prosper'. I just lean into His loving arms and soak in His love and peace. I tell Jesus I don't want to leave here, but He says I have to. There is much I need to do, but we will come back here many times.

8‑ 8‑ 8‑

VELMA
3/ 28/
Ribboned

"Here I am to worship. Here I am to bow down. Here I am to say that You're my God . . . .The Path welcomes me today joining in with my song. Path wraps Itself around me like a huge ribbon, caressing me as we sing. "I'll never know how much it cost to see my sin upon that cross." Path (Holy Spirit) can't join me in that phrase. He knows very well the price that was paid. From before time began, He knows. As He continues caressing me, He imparts more understanding of His knowledge to me. He guides me into all truth. He reveals hidden secrets. He points at Jesus and says, "Behold the Lamb of God."

The Lamb comes walking toward us and joins our dance of worship. I am encapsulated as Holy Spirit loves The Lamb, The Lamb loves Holy Spirit and they both love me. Only thoughts of pure love are being released, washing me, inexplicably building me. Holy Spirit isn't just wrapping around us, He's lacing through us—binding us together. Each time He weaves through us, we attach to Him and are woven into the other, integrated, inseparable. Jesus in me. Me in Jesus. Holy Spirit in both of us. We are inseparable. I am reminded of the various unbreakable covenants:

- The Salt Covenant because you cannot separate the grains of salt back into their original pouches.
- The Blood Covenant because you cannot separate the blood once it mingles or restore it once it's shed.
- The Word Covenant because God will not go back on His Word.

We are not separate. When we partake of His body and His blood—we are inseparable. *Lord, help me to receive and walk in the fullness of this.*

We are no longer standing face to face, The Lamb and I. He is behind me and I am reminded that the Glory of the Lord is my rearguard. Holy Spirit begins lacing our heads together, working quickly, and I know something else is happening. Quickly, quickly Holy Spirit moves lacing my head to My Lord's head. Now Holy Spirit begins lacing my feet through nail holes in The Lamb's feet. I realize when He laced our heads together it was the crown of thorns.

Weeping I speak. "Lord, take me back to the crown of thorns. I don't want to be sheltered from what You did for me. Please, Holy Spirit, take me back to the crown." My face is intricately laced through as His beard was pulled from His face. My cheeks are interwoven as I see the bruising from the beating. Holy Spirit works more slowly as He lays himself carefully in each stripe on My Master's back, piercing through me at each point where rock, bone and metal ripped flesh from My Lord. I find the lashes were not confined to His shoulders, but extend down to His hips. Here comes a lash wrapping around over my right shoulder. Another wraps around cutting into my chest.

I feel the Heart of the Lamb as in His pain His thoughts turn to those wielding the whips. At first they thought nothing of this, just another lesson for the Jews. As the first lash ripped flesh from

148

the Lamb of God, their hearts were ripped with anguish as well. "Oh, Lord! Forgive these men!" My heart cries with the Heart of The Lamb. Here comes one at my hips, wrapping around ripping flesh from my abdomen, another at my waist wraps and rips into my stomach.

In anguish I cry out:

"RIBBONED! I AM RIBBONED!"

Moving on now, swiftly again, my knees are laced to The Lamb as He fell under the weight of the cross. Unable to catch Himself, His shoulders are bruised and His head bounces off the cobblestones as the thorns pierce even more deeply into His flesh—yes—even into His skull. His hands remain on the cross He is bearing, exposing His elbows to the rocky road. His shoulders seem to be dislocated by the fall. His jawbone dislocates as His chin hits the ground.

My hands are laced to His hands through the nail holes. First, my left hand, the Law; then my right, relationship. His body already racked with pain, this new invasion pierces through the unspeakable pain like white-hot pokers from the fires of hell. Now, one nail in His feet. My feet are laced to His.

As the spear is thrust through His side, piercing the liver, lungs and heart, the pain is different. It is not experienced physically because His body has already kissed death—but—He— experiences the pain of each of those watching who love Him. This pain is more extended, for this body can't absorb it and move on. As long as the heart of those who love Him hurts, the heart of The Lamb hurts as well.

In addition, the heart of The Lamb longs for those who walk by without seeing Him as He cries out from beyond the cross. His heart breaks as they search without seeing, ask without hearing, speak without knowing and long without fulfillment. The Lamb is encouraged and His heart gladdened when they acknowledge Him—reach out to Him. Love pours forth, warming their hearts, encouraging them and extending His favor toward them as He woos them by His Spirit.

I stand, wrapped in The Lamb of God, My flesh laced through with His flesh. My heart longing for others as His heart longs. "Lord, how does one go on from this place?"

"You go on in ME, My Beloved. By My Spirit. You go on in Me."

ᴏ— ᴏ— ᴏ—

FRAN S.
2007
The Struggle

I'm aware of the beautiful morning. The beauty seems to seep into my receptors. (On a previous visit He taught me that 'receptors' were like the very pores on my body and would receive what He was presenting—even to the point of enlarging them as if under a microscope.) On occasion, yesterday's thoughts said, "Could this be a looking into the Spirit's world and watching at the same time? I wasn't able to make the move then. You know I always go straight to 'business,' Lord. Sorry," I said, "Although, I know I'm not in your way. Holy Spirit, help me!! Oh how I love my Three Layer Rock."

"Everyone has a Three Layer Rock," He says, as my thoughts had just asked the question.

"I wonder if everyone"….my thoughts were put aside as He said, "Put your fingertips up to mine." I see me doing this. Now He clasps them with HIS fingers entwined in mine. We struggle. I'm actually fighting Him and pushing Him away. I'm in emotional

150

pain, needing help, but fighting against His holding onto me, not in a fighting way, but a holding way to prevent me from hurting myself. I see myself finally tire and begin to collapse. He then gently lays me down on my side, almost in a heap on a beautiful green hillside. Then He sits, reclines, facing me waiting for me to recover. I don't seem to have the energy to even look at Him even though I know He's there. "What does this mean?" my thoughts say. Then Jesus speaks gently to me responding to my thoughts, "Like I told you before, I will take care of you. I died for you."

I seem to be getting strength back—His? I wonder. He smiles. I move toward Him and rest my head on His knee as He reclines but doesn't come to me. I move to Him.

In the distance on many other green hills I could hear sheep in various stages of being. He's with all of them, too. Then I become aware of an area of traffic to my right. It's like a 'herd' of people moving down the hill we're on, headed toward the well. They aren't looking in our direction. They don't have eyes to see us yet.

"Much is going on that you don't have eyes to see, Love," my precious Jesus says. "OH MY!" My thoughts exclaim. "Well, let's go join them," He says. It seems my strength has been totally renewed. We just blend in and proceed with "the herd." "The herd" is pleased, eager, joyful, excited about getting to the well. They've been there before, He lets me know, that's the reason you feel all these things about them, and you recognize it because you, too, have been there. "OH MY! Yes!" My thoughts again.

The stream of people begins to slow as they mill around the well, no one is upset that they aren't right next to the well. All have a perfect vantage point. Now, I'm aware that Jesus has come out of the crowd, and set Himself down on the well curb. The rest of us sit on the ground of the grassy hill. That gives us the advantage of an amphitheater sitting view. He begins speaking and we hang on every word, absorbing them into our receptors. We are being equipped. We love it. "This must have been what it was like in the New Testament writings of You." "YES"! There goes my mind again, and His response. I hope we're here for hours or even days as we absorb.

Night is falling. He waves His hand over the crowd and we take rest, right where we are. OH MY!! Jesus sits in front of the well and leans His back against the wall and rests. Now I shut my eyes. "Oh how I love You, my Three Layer Rock."

⸗ ⸗ ⸗

SANDRA M.
The Great Sadness
I have held onto a deep sadness over the past several years. As I was waiting on the Lord, He took me to the depths of my soul. The 'ground' was covered with a sludgy, black, rocky, muck substance—representing my deep sadness. I was holding a shovel—trying to shovel it out—but there's nowhere to put it. I am crying. Then I see Jesus standing near. I think to myself, "Yay— He's here! He will make it all go away!!" But He just stands there.

I try handing Him the shovel, but He shakes His head and just stands there with a little grin on His face.

I begin really crying now, continuing to try to shovel the muck. The tears are falling to the ground—I begin to see the muck dissolving as the tears fall onto it. At that point the Lord says to me, "This will only go away through repentance."

I then realized that I was holding on to my sadness—as though I was entitled to it—due it. Once I repented of holding onto sadness—it completely disappeared.

⸗ ⸗ ⸗

152

VELMA
9/20

A Cleansing

This morning the voice of My Lord wakes me. "I want to talk with you."

As I sit down at the computer The Path welcomes my feet and I stand for a while, just delighting in being there. The Path kisses my toes then rises up and wraps around me. I physically feel warmth on my back—around and between my shoulders—relaxing my muscles and removing tension I didn't even know I had. My spine begins to align properly releasing the sinews in my neck. I hear Holy Spirit (The Path) saying, "I love you." I am so thrilled as Holy Spirit hugs me as you would a tender baby. "We have much to do today. We are happy you have chosen to spend time with Us. Your beloved is waiting at the Well." This long, wonderful hug deposits me right in front of My Beloved. Holy Spirit always takes me to Jesus.

My Lord is standing quietly by the well, dressed in white on white riding clothes and I am surprised to realize that I am dressed like Him. I know the undergarment is simple and I am caught by the honor it enjoys resting directly on His skin. The sleeves are long, the neck rounded; I know that the garment is seamless. The outer garment is the same kind of material, soft and light though quite thick. It buttons downward to mid thigh in the front. The sides are split up to His waist. The sleeves are slightly shorter than the sleeves of the undergarment and the length is about two inches shorter than the undergarment which rests on the toes of His white riding boots. A simple gold crown rests on His laughing hair today.

He's smiling as He watches me with The Path of The Spirit and as I am deposited in front of Him, He reaches for the tips of my fingers of my left hand. I bask in His smile. Even with my eyes closed, I can see His loving eyes embracing my face. As He pulls me to Himself, His left hand caresses my head and He kisses my left temple.

As He holds me, I hear, "Flesh and blood cannot inherit the Kingdom." Instantly, I'm taken to the resurrection and see the transformation of physical body to heavenly substance as life awakens His body and He passes from the grave to the garden. I actually see the touch that glorifies His flesh! It seems to burst from the marrow of His bones and my eyes are inside Him watching the transformation! What a glorious privilege! What an honor to witness this with my eyes inside His mortal body actually witnessing mortal becoming immortal! Earthly becoming Heavenly! Death being abolished by LIFE! As this is happening I am fully aware this will happen to me—to us who remain. Can it be that it is beginning to happen even now? When did it happen for Enoch? Elijah? Moses? I know graves have already been emptied at His resurrection. Were those who rose transformed at that time? "CERTAINLY," (I hear).

"To walk where you've been appointed to walk, you must be changed physically as well as spiritually," My Lord whispers as the wonder of transformation is revealed. I release myself to His will—to transformation. I desire it to be instantaneous. I feel energy coursing through my flesh. I sense that some of my flesh is being judged. I'm not talking soul—I'm talking "flesh." (Perhaps it's bacteria and such.) I feel my brain "shift" as if moved, repositioned in my skull. I feel pain in different areas—areas in which I know I've had problems, sinuses, and back. I feel coolness in my right foot as in other parts of my body.

All the while, My Lord holds me infusing me with His virtue—the power that raised Him from the dead—the heavenly substance. (Dare I believe? Lord I believe! Help my unbelief!) I release myself more fully to His grace. His mercy comforts me. I expect to feel energized but my body feels weighed down. I see holes as if chunks have been removed from me. Thank You, Lord.

My spine pops again. This time a little lower down, below my shoulder blades.

Now we sit on the curb of the well and as I drink from the silver ladle, the glorious light of His presence spills out of me like water through a sieve. I smile and sense that my whole body smiles. I must really look surprised because My Lord throws His head back and laughs.

OH!

THE GLORIOUS SOUND OF HIS LAUGHTER! I LOVE IT!

᚛ ᚛ ᚛

SANDRA M.
Soaring With the Eagle

This encounter occurred during a great time of stress and change in my life.

I was laying on a grassy hill under some oak trees just basking in the warmth of the sun. Jesus was sitting next to a tree near me. I saw an eagle soaring over head and just watched it as it swooped down and picked me up in His talons. He flew higher and higher and then dropped me. I began falling—but had no fear as I knew His eye was on me.

He let me fall for a little while and then swooped down and repositioned me on His back. We soared again up into the sky. I asked, "Him where are you taking me?" He did not answer—but flew me up to the side of rocky, crag mountain high up above the timber line. He set me down on a ledge there and He told me to rest here, and that He would nurture me and take care of me, then He flew off. I felt so relieved, as I was in much need of rest and solitude.

After some time, He came back and took me again upon His back. We soared down into a lush green valley with a beautiful river running through it. He set me down next to the river and said "I want you to drink from this river—it is the River of Life."

I knelt down to scoop up a handful of water, but the next thing I knew, I was in the middle of the river laying on my back and the water was rushing over me—my mouth was open and it was pouring into me. It felt so incredibly refreshing. I got back up onto the river bank and
my whole being seemed to be translucent and glowing. It was such an incredible feeling. Next the Eagle took me again on His back. We flew quite a long distance and came upon a very thick black burnt out forest. He set me upon a branch and sat next to me in the pitch darkness and asked, "How do you feel?"

I responded, "I feel great!"

He asked me, "Why?"

I said, "Because, I am full of LIFE!" . . .He grinned and nodded.

(Several months after that I left my job of 23 years as a church secretary—leaving behind many, many dear friends, ministries—my 'life as I knew it'—and moved up into an isolated forest which actually experienced a fire the following year. The Lord had prepared my heart and my spirit for this new life. He is nurturing and taking care of me.)

❧ ❧ ❧

DIANA M.
2007
Let It All Go
We listened to praise and the love of the Holy Spirit music captured us as we entered the time of visitation with our Lord Jesus.

God, I know you are disciplining me for something great. It

is so hard to watch loved ones hurt but I know you can heal their hurts and I can't. I am probably contributing to some of their hurts. Holy Spirit, I need you to stay real close to me and let God's love keep flowing through me so that the lies of satan and people's criticism don't harm Your love in me. Oh, Lord, how I love and need this time with you and ones of like mind and the harmony here. It keeps me able to get through the week knowing Your love is really for me too. I finally believe it, know it and feel it with no doubts. Help me to always stay as close to You as possible with nothing separating us.

We are flying together through the air and the look of happiness and acceptance of being loved just like I am is just beaming on my face as we fly through the air together, hand in hand. The look of love on my Lord's face just makes me feel like I never have before. No matter what, He loves me just the way I am and we whirl around in circles and laugh on and on as we fly together. It is so awesome. The freedom and the peace just go on and on as we fly together. It is so awesome. This freedom is so overwhelming I feel like I could burst but don't want it to end either.

As I was praying in the spirit, the Lord kept telling me to let it all go, let it all go. I said, "Well, my paper will fall and my pen."

Jesus said, "Let it all go."

I fought that for a while and finally I gave in. I was slain in the spirit and while I was slain in the Spirit, He kept telling me not to worry about what He wanted me to do and if I didn't have the ability to do it that He would take care of all that and to just obey Him and take the step in faith. I was slain in the spirit for quite some time and it was wonderful and then I came to and we went on with our wonderful meeting with Lord and the Holy Spirit, sharing our experiences from the time of visitation.

GROUP EXPERIENCE
June 10
ANGELIC VISITOR

On June 3, during our time of visitation, the Lord had told me He was going to permit "a group visit." That day, there were five people with me so I expected it would include all who were there. I didn't understand exactly what He meant and had no idea when it would happen so I said nothing to the group.

This group visit occurred the following Sunday, June 10th. There were only two others with me that day. We each perceived the events somewhat differently just as we all do when we see things from different perspective in the natural. To be able to relate the complete experience, I've included their perspectives punctuated with my mine.

* * *

FRAN:

This Sunday, again, was a wonderful time of study. As we each share with one another it's another opportunity to learn how God moves in our lives and how THE WORD applies to our everyday experiences.

Somewhere around 5:30 p.m. it seemed things were coming to an ending. I told Velma I was going to leave. She had always expressed to everyone who came that we could stay as long as we wanted. She said, "OK, but just so you know there's an angelic presence between your chair and the door." This information was given as I seem to receive quite easily and quickly. Sure enough, my ability to stand wilted into a crawl as the path to the exit just couldn't be navigated. So I decided to stay. (Who would want to leave this Presence?) I again tried to stand while holding onto a table on one side and Velma holding me on the other.

During this period I had a vision of a piece of paper about the size of a typing paper. It was folded in half and began to fly upward from my presence like a bird might fly. The paper was blank on the inside. Almost immediately several of these folded flying pieces joined this one and they took on a formation as geese and other birds of flight do on long cross country trips. It was beautiful. I finally sat back down.

(My perspective: When Fran first entered the sphere of the angelic visitor, she began to crumble. Diana and I rushed to keep her head from hitting the floor. We were able to get her back to her chair where we "draped" her on the chair. Her back was to the visitor and her arms draped over the back of the chair so she wouldn't fall again. During that brief time, she saw the cards flying. Fran had recently begun creating greeting cards of various types. She explained to us later that each card had its own destination to touch a soul.)

At some point Velma just hurried into the area in mention and began to 'splash' about with such joy telling the Lord she wanted to receive everything in His Presence that had been sent.

(My perspective: I asked Diana if she wanted to step up next. She said she would wait, so I stepped up with what I thought to be a reverential attitude. (Evidently, not so from Fran's perspective in the Spirit realm.) Immediately the wind in the presence of the visitor began buffeting me and, though I tried with all my might to stay still, I felt like a flag on a windy day. Fran, still with her back to the visitor and me said, "Tsunami." When she said that, the wind increased to greater intensity and became a straight wind, blowing me rapidly across the room to deposit me at Diana's feet. She was sitting on the couch and I expected to be blown on top of her. Instead, the wind stopped suddenly and I was able to step away and take my seat. At some point before the tsunami blew me out of the presence, I received verbal instructions

from the angel and was given a scroll.)

FRAN:

Diana had not experienced this type of visitation and was sitting on the sofa. Velma said, "Would you like to come over and stand in this presence?" She said sure. I heard in my spirit, she doesn't believe she'll receive anything, even though it's obvious to her you all have, but she's willing because Velma asked.

Wow, when she got to the area, my recall is that she was having trouble standing. I believe Velma tried to help hold her. I remember thinking tsunami is coming to Dianna. (I may have said this aloud.) About this time Dianna very quickly as though being swept, began to travel backward until the sofa caught her and she was overcome in the Spirit. (Later she said she had not expected to receive anything as she thought she didn't know enough nor had she been around spiritual movement.)

There was much more and this took much longer to happen than it does to tell, because it was now 7:30pm.

DIANA:

After we read our trips to each other, Velma says, "There is a very large angel between the table and the hall, but we just kept talking.

(My perspective: I told them we needed to pray in the spirit and see how we were to respond to this visitor.)

Then Fran got up to tell a story about Victor and Velma's ministries coming together and she got in the angel's space and she just went limp and we had to catch her. Velma prayed that whatever reason the angel was there that we would all get the revelation.

Velma then got up and walked into the angel's space and

she became weak and limp and then Fran said "It is just like a tsunami," and Velma came flying out of the angel's space.

She (Velma) then said for me to try it and I have to be honest, I didn't think anything would happen. But, when I walked through that angel's space I was limp. My legs gave way and I had to hold onto the table and the wall to keep from falling and I just kept holding on and then all of a sudden, I was thrown backwards out of that place.

We prayed and talked some more and Fran began to pray in the spirit and prophesy and she laid hands on me and prayed in the spirit and made beep, beep and boop bop noises and the spirit of laughter fell on me and I laughed and then we all began to laugh. We laughed for a long time and then we tried to leave and we all got hit with laughter again and it took us quite a while to get out the door and to the elevator and down to the cars. We had to help each other walk. It was absolutely wonderful.

We were all drunk in the spirit and it was wonderful and hilarious. Fran was crawling on the floor trying to get out of the apartment and Velma and I were laughing so hard and Velma finally got her up but it was so funny. She was trying to lift her leg and it would just wiggle and we laughed so hard. This was before we got out of the door of the apartment

(My perspective: When Fran tried to leave my apartment, as she approached the place where the angelic visitor had been, she crumpled to the floor. She had to get home because her husband expected her around six and it was already seven thirty. She began crawling and was able to maneuver the turn into the hall but was unable to get up. Diana and I tried to help her but she said she needed to get her legs under her by herself so she would be able to stand.

She finally reached the coat closet door and began pulling herself up by the doorjamb. She was able to get her right leg in a squatting position but her left leg took more effort. She could only pull it up about an inch at a time and it would tremble and shake then another inch and so on. It took her quite some time to get both legs under her. Then she allowed me to help her walk.

Diana was carrying both their purses and Bibles. By the time we got to Fran's car she seemed able to handle herself well enough to drive home. She later told me she had to plan her stops because it took her two blocks to get her foot up on the brake.

Each of us received instruction and impartation from the angelic encounter. We praised God and thanked Him for loving us so much and for allowing us to experience this group encounter with a heavenly visitor. We were all changed that day and became more stable in our assignments.)

Fran was still under the influence of the Spirit the next day when we met to go to a prayer meeting. She later told me the effect lasted a few days.

Diana told us later that she had remained under the influence of that visitation for three days. She was unable to walk straight and would have to aim her left shoulder toward the direction she needed to go.

⊷ ⊷ ⊷

FRAN S.
6/11
Purpose

Thank you Father for allowing a visitation of your strength yesterday at Velma's. Purpose is wonderful. I'm BEING today and heading for the Bible study at Benton. Help us have just what you need us to have.

Where do you want me today? I believe I inhaled your fragrance today. Like sweet flowers. Oh Precious One, My Three Layer Rock. Thank You All for hugging me today. I love You. Precious are You. Great joy I receive and desire to pass on so others may know.

Then He began to speak in that still small voice. "Continue to press into me. Continue to receive everything I present to you. Watch and listen. Watch and listen in both worlds every day. It will become natural. You're not calling things that are not as though they were. The world I'm in is the real world. You're flesh is walking in a nugget of time attached to the wall of your spiritual walk. A thin membrane is between where you are in your nugget and the spirit world. Keep looking in the spirit direction and punching at the membrane that separates us at times. I came into your world yesterday by knowing the membrane was nonexistent to Me. Then, you three walked in My world of knowing, strength, receiving and love, love, love with purpose. You thought you were done at 5:30 your time, but My precious one needed to talk and you could see and understand I take advantage of her regularly and she loves it. You also understood that she is one of the people I use to help children that are hurting. (He was speaking of Diana) She won't give up."

My mind has a question. "While in Your presence yesterday, my seeing the handmade cards, did I grasp that in part at least, that you need those done." (Just as I said these words, I again saw a card unfold and fly. Then I saw there was a flying stream of them through the sky.) I asked, "The one I saw, Lord, was blank. What does that mean? That they're new and ready to be filled at a moment's notice? OK!" I said, "I understand."

Then He seems to indicate for me to get lots of them made up. He says, "I will inspire the inside—but you'll be ready when that comes."

"OK, I'll go with that," my mind says.

"The handkerchiefs, too, are part of Me. Walk in both worlds today as much as you can receive." He continues.

"OK! I can receive that."

"Here's another drink, but let Me tip it up at the end. It's much sweeter that way. I know how long to let it take, like yesterday," He finishes.

"I love You. Thank You, My Three Layer Rock." Oh my, this sure sends one into a wonderful day, alive and full of Him.

⊶ ⊶ ⊶

FRAN S
6/4
Spiritual House

Our journey is already in the Presence of the Father. The Son holds me and displays my blue mantel and draws me to Him for comfort.

"Come to Me so I may bless you and teach you more things and revelations, that My work may continue through you whenever I need it to be." He said to me, "I love you so much, I would show you Myself even if for no other reason but to love you. I have much for you to understand. It is not hard. It is very revealing for more and more steps for you to understand.

"Don't place your looks upon man. Always ask Me and confide in Me. I will always give you an answer. You must just listen, for it can come in many, many different ways. You may need to talk less to people and listen more from Me. More study. Place your looking toward Me. Listen, listen, listen.

"Ask the Holy Spirit to teach, teach, teach you My

mysteries. It is important. There isn't time to tell you what all is involved in the furtherance of My Kingdom just from you. (I believe that meant whatever times He might need or use me.) Do not rise above yourself so you can hear me. Precious are you to me!"

"You do have a house with me and it does have a drive-up window for those who are soooo hungry and don't know where to go for their needs. Then they see a flashing light that shows them the drive-up window to **E A T**. And it's got 'stuff' that will keep them coming back until they know how to choose various houses to visit and **S I P**."

"Thank You, Holy Spirit," I said.

"Just love My people with My love and compassion that they will be so tender and the Holy Spirit can draw them and bring them to Me."

(Velma, this happened Monday night this week. I had such an intense love for everyone there. I wanted to touch, hold, pat, love on them and look into their eyes until they seemed to break open. WOW!)

"Come to the Well of My Presence often, often, often."

᚛— ᚛— ᚛—

VELMA
4/9

The Mountain School
I'm headed for The Path! How exciting! Path still laps a good way down the hill; guess I'll have to come here more often to build my strength. (The Path recedes up the hill as my strength increases. Then, when I'm accustomed to that level, the hill grows and Path extends down to help me increase my strength again.)

"I love You Lord." I'm looking around and see hills on my right, my left and behind me of various sizes and differing angle of slope. Of course I'm unable to see past the hill I'm on so cannot see what's in front of me. I saw The Path in front of me but don't know if I stepped on it or not. I find myself on the plateau in the Alp-like mountains. (This is one of my favorite places to visit.) The air is crisp—pristine. I'm wearing a long white dress with matching cloak. They are heavy wool and trimmed in soft white fur as are my muff and hat. The small white tent (of Holy Spirit) is behind me, its flaps moving gently in the breeze.

"It's a beautiful day today," My Lord speaks as He approaches me. His voice is full of life and carries a flavor of accomplishment. I sense He's been working this morning. "Yes," He responds to my thoughts. "I have something to show you today." He's dressed in white as well but His sleeves are rolled up to about three-quarter length. He takes my elbow and we begin walking toward the snow capped mountain on the north.

There is neither bridge nor path that leads over to the next mountain. When we reach the edge of the plateau we're on, we continue walking on . . . nothing. As we approach the shear, rock, mountain, I see a door has been carved into its side. We pause, standing on . . . nothing. My Lord hands me an ancient looking key. It's ornately carved of silver, tarnished from lack of use. As He hands me the key, the door in the side of the mountain slides open.

The interior is already lighted by torches fastened in nooks in the walls. From here, it looks as though the entire mountain has been carved out and only the shell remains to enclose what has been created here. My Lord is excited as He points out how the carving has been done; the different marks made by various tools that were used to hew the stone.

There is a stream running through a large open room and

we follow it to its source, a huge rock from which the water bubbles forth like a fountain about four feet high. The water is crystal clear but with a slight blue tint. I turn to face My Lord.

"This is a place for learning. This is the water of life. It comes forth from The Rock—You," I declare.

"Yes, Beloved. Your senses are becoming sharpened. The more you depend upon My Spirit, the more you will see, hear and understand. There are many things here you have not yet perceived. You must walk into the next room alone."

I turn to see the next room. There is nothing but darkness ahead of me. I cannot even see the walls of this cavern nor in what direction to go. I turn back to My Lord. He simply smiles and I believe I see a slight dare in His eyes.

Well! That's all I need! He's here. He will never leave me nor forsake me. If He is for me who can be against me? What harm can come to me when I'm under His watch care? I turn back to the darkness, take a deep breath and close my eyes. *Holy Spirit, You are my guide. You guide me into all truth. You teach me all things. Show me the truth of what lies ahead.*

When I open my eyes, I see the room is well lighted. I look for the source of light, turning this way then that. Tch! IT'S ME! At this realization, the light becomes brighter but the room still appears to be empty except for me. *Holy Spirit, open my eyes so I can see and my ears so I can hear. Open my heart so I can understand.*

As I pray, my eyes are opened to see a large table spread with a feast: turkey, fresh fruit, flowers, cakes, soup, vegetables— everything. The people around the table are all talking, some motioning with their forks or spoons, others pointing with a partially eaten turkey leg. There is red wine in the glasses and pitchers of crystal clear water, no blue tint here. I see a large Bible on a side table. It has a gold cross embossed on the front.

These people are all dressed in frontier style clothes. The man at the end of the table, evidently the leader, catches sight of me out of the corner of his eye. He is very startled, scooting back—knocking his chair over as he turns to face me.

"What are YOU doing here? What do you want from us?" he asks with a cut of distrust in his voice.

"Sir, I don't know you. I want nothing of you. I am simply observing."

"You people never come to just observe. There's always something you want to change about us every time. **Well**, we **are** Christian you know. We **do** serve God. He **is** a recognized part of our daily lives."

"Oh. Others like me have come here?"

"Yes, from time to time. They have been few, but they have come."

"Has anyone ever given you the light?"

"The light? What light? We have light," he responds as he holds up the Bible.

"You are sitting in darkness. Do you not want the light of revelation? Do you not desire the light of understanding and wisdom?"

I can see on his face, as he lays the Bible aside, that he doesn't really understand and in a vision I see him stepping through the granite door and being blinded by the Sonshine. I know Holy Spirit is telling me to lead them carefully so they do not retreat further into darkness.

I step to the side table and pick up the Bible. I begin reading from Luke chapter 4:

Luke 4:18:
The Spirit of the Lord [is] upon me, because he hath anointed me to preach the gospel to the poor; he hath sent me to heal the brokenhearted, to preach deliverance to the captives, and recovering of sight to the blind, to set at liberty them that are bruised,

Luke 4:19:
To preach the acceptable year of the Lord.

Then I turn to Matthew chapter 4:

Matthew 4:16:
The people which sat in darkness saw great a light; and to them which sat in the region and shadow of death light is sprung up.

Matthew 4:17:
From that time Jesus began to preach, and to say, Repent: for the kingdom of heaven is at hand.

Next I turn to Luke chapter 17:

Luke 17:20:
And when he was demanded of the Pharisees, when the kingdom of God should come, he answered them and said, The kingdom of God cometh not with observation:

Luke 17:21:
Neither shall they say, Lo here! or, lo there! for, behold, the kingdom of God is within you.

"I have come to encourage you not to be satisfied with what you have always known. I have come to give you a taste of something more." (I give each of them a mustard seed, an impartation of wisdom and understanding that as they watch the mustard seed become all it can be, they will begin desiring to be all they can be as well.)

As I turn to go, the leader—still looking at the tiny seed in his hand says, "Wait! There is much we need to know about this seed."

I hand him the Bible, "Read this again with a willingness to see what you haven't seen, to understand what you have not understood, to hear what you have not heard before. It will give you the light you need for the seed to grow. Plant your seed in this Book."

I walk to the entrance of this room. I wonder if I have left enough light to allow them to see. I turn and look back. The Bible, now open in front of the leader is glowing and lighting the room. His voice reaches me as he reads:

Isaiah 11:1:
And there shall come forth a rod out of the stem of Jesse, and a Branch shall grow out of his roots:

Isaiah 11:2:
And the spirit of the LORD shall rest upon him, the spirit of wisdom and understanding, the spirit of counsel and might, the spirit of knowledge and of the fear of the LORD;

Isaiah 11:3:
And shall make him of quick understanding in the fear of the LORD: and he shall not judge after the sight of his eyes, neither reprove after the hearing of his ears:

Isaiah 11:4

But with righteousness shall he judge the poor, and reprove with equity for the meek of the earth: and he shall smite the earth with the rod of his mouth, and with the breath of his lips shall he slay the wicked.

Isaiah 11:5

And righteousness shall be the girdle of his loins, and faithfulness the girdle of his reins.

As I step back through the entrance to this room, I practically bump into My Lord. I had just been thinking that I sensed His presence with me but there was no light beside me nor behind me. "That's because I was IN you. Did I not tell you that the Father and I would make our abode in you?"

"You know You did, Lord. I see much has to change in my perception as well as theirs. Oh, Lord, I feel like a different person. I like this place."

"You will find many surprises here. You have done well on this day. You did not rush on with the giftings within you. You heard the voice of My Spirit cautioning you and you took them back to the sure foundation of My Word. Tomorrow will be a new experience. Take your time as you work through this mountain school. There are pitfalls of the ancients, there are illusions, there will be serpents and wolves in sheep's clothing. You must depend on My Spirit at all times. Things are rarely as they first appear."

He hands me a chisel and a hammer to "write" my experience on the wall. As I look around for a space to write, I see that in this area there is only one space not already covered with writing. The blank space is about twelve feet high and eight feet wide. All the writings cover approximately the same amount of space. The writing differs in size and style. I don't know how to "write" with a chisel and hammer, but I begin. By the time I'm finished the entire space is covered in writing, though I don't not know how I got to the top of my space, nor do I remember lying down to write at the bottom. Still, it is all covered with words.

Now, the Lord and I are walking across the space between this mountain and the plateau where the small white tent still sits, open and inviting.

"Enter into the tent. You will find rest there and the air will refresh you." My Lord embraces me, infusing me with peace, joy, love, wisdom, contentment—then releases me to the tent.

As I enter the tent, I see cushions of various bright colors where I lie down. *Not what I expected. I thought everything in here would be white!* Holy Spirit envelopes me as His rest lulls me to sleep.

⊷ ⊷ ⊷

VELMA
9/20
Perspective

I'm hearing "Ride! Quickly Ride!"

I see that horses have been brought to us. I wonder who this is who so patiently waits holding the reins of the horses as my Lord and I sit laughing together. I almost get distracted wanting to know his name, knowing that everyone in this realm is worthy of honor. By concentrating on wanting to know the name of this smiling servant, I nearly fail to acknowledge seeing the transformation of the land here or perhaps, my ability to see some things. Flowers have decorated the short grass and the little animals are gathered around watching us. As we walk toward the horses, My Lord takes the reins of His horse and at the same time hugs the page as a father would his teenage son. (Actually like He did me as he pulled my head against His shoulder.) I am surprised to find myself on my

172

horse.

The horses are beautiful, like Lipizzaner stallions, perfectly white—their coats so smooth—their muzzles so soft—their eyes adoring their Master. The reins are gold and silver, studded with precious gems. The saddles are the same but padded with some kind of marvelous substance that makes me feel one with the horse. The feel reminds me of the gel-seats cross country truck drivers use.

This is a new experience for me. Of course, no two visits have been the same here, but I've never ridden a horse with Him before. I'm on His left as we start out but as we arrive at our destination—Earth. I am on His right.

We stop in the heavens and view earth. I'm sure this is what it looks like from the space station, so surreal. At first, it looks beautiful and peaceful and I am blessed looking at it. Suddenly there is an explosion! "It's Alaska! LORD! What do we do? How do we pray?!"

"They're trying to cripple your nation."

I don't see explosions in the continental states, just Alaska. Now I see five explosions in Siberia! "THE OILFIELDS! LORD! SHOULD I TELL!? WHO SHOULD I TELL?!"

I see one huge explosion in China. Now Argentina! Now in Central Africa! Why would they hit Puerto Rico! I must not get distracted! I'm with the King of Kings, Creator of the Universe! I must be ready to see this or He would not have brought me here. *Calm down, Velma. Calm down. He's just watching, showing me things to come. Calm down.* My horse has sensed my agitation and stamps its front feet, trying to force the bit from its mouth. I realize I've pulled the reins tight. I relax and the horse settles down.

Lord, teach me to pray. Holy Spirit—guide me in everything I do and say.

I'm aware that I haven't seen armies with us this time. It's just me and My Lord. O.K. O.K. I must not miss anything. I do see a host of angels above us. They are watchers, swords drawn but not "at the ready." They are looking on as we are.

Have I already missed something? I look at My Lord. His eyes are shooting out laser beams toward earth and I am able to see into a jungle in the center of the South American continent, troops with military hand weapons (no tanks or bazookas or anything like that). They are not wearing helmets but rather are wearing billed caps, not like baseball caps, taller and made of khaki material. I can even see their eyes and how they have their combat boots tied. I wonder what they're after?

"Wars are coming to the earth; unprecedented by previous wars. Life in every nation will change. People will become more unified in their thoughts though not in purpose. The proliferation of their thoughts of danger and of war, of hatred and fear will cause those things to propagate so that what they fear will come upon them.

"My People must become wise. They must be wise as the serpent but gentle in their thoughts. In days to come, fear will expose them to the enemy, but a mind stayed on Me will cover them as though in a cave. My people must enter My rest as the danger increases. They must have a view of their dual citizenship—earth and heaven. That is why I am releasing experiential books into their hands. Those of you who spend time with Me as you are will find their mind stayed on Me in crisis times. They will not be swayed by what they see. They will not betray their children."

"It is not yet time to sound the alarm. It is a time to call others to communion with ME. You must let them know I long to talk with them as friend talks with friend. My heart longs to be joined with them."

As He said this I saw red "cords" shoot from His heart to people all over the globe. I saw faces turned up to receive—His glory gracing their countenance. People from every nation, loving His attention, experiencing His touch. I see Buddhist monks having "Damascus Road experiences." A group walking along together in their orange robes and large hats. Two being knocked down by the power of God as My Lord reveals Himself to them.

There's the Tibetan monk I've seen before, on the balcony of the monastery seeing the 'Great Light.' "Yes, he has been waiting decades, knowing there was more but not knowing how to access Me."

I see a voodoo priest electrified as he sees the Living God. I see statues falling on their faces as Dagon did before the Ark. I see Eskimos warmed by Light that invades their homes.

"So, You're showing me that during this time of unprecedented war there will also be unprecedented visitations." (As I'm thinking this I am able to know the end of my thought and His response before I complete my thought!)

"Yes, and even prior to the beginning of war My Body will begin manifesting My Kingdom on earth." (As He says this, I see individuals surrounded with the substance from the depth of the Well of His Presence. I can feel the thickness of His Presence around them and see it as huge bubbles of light. Though it is still day, this light is brighter than day.)

"Lord, I'm comforted to see that it is still day, for Your Word says there will come a time of darkness when no man can work."

"Times of darkness have already come and more will occur. My works must multiply on earth. Guard those through whom they come. They must be guarded in times of rest as well as times of works. They must learn to preserve themselves. I have need of their physical bodies while it is yet the Time of Man."

Looking back to earth, I see an outpost on the North Pole, a smaller one on the South Pole. I am amused that those on the North Pole think they're on the top and those on the South Pole think they are. Everyone is on the top! Because, from any direction, up is still up!

I see the leaders of violence, leaders of violent nations, filled with hatred. They are sons of Cain, sons of disobedience, full of themselves, becoming their own god. They don't believe in the god of their peoples. They believe they are the god of their people. They spill out wickedness even with their eyes.

In contrast, I see the leaders of passive nations. These leaders have knowledge of God, the true God, but have no motivation to seek Him out.

The violent are a tool to turn people's hearts to God. I see leaders of peaceful nations, sustained for generations by the prayers of their Christian peoples, suddenly collapse (hats falling off), falling to their knees realizing that the prayers of their people aren't enough, THEY need God themselves, for themselves, not just as a leader (that's why their hats fell off), but as any other needy person. They must meet God themselves, daily, face to face. Without the threat of eminent danger, they would go on with their lukewarm lives, sustained only by duty.

"Come," He says as our horses turn and begin running through the universe. What joy on His face as we race! I hear His thoughts. "Soon. Soon we will all be together. We will be one." I know He's talking about ALL the heirs of salvation, His family! We race on, laughing together, Spirit Wind sometimes catching my breath, catching me by surprise! I love it!

(I was permitted to release this visitation to appropriate leaders a few years later.)

DARE TO BELIEVE YOU CAN BE GREAT IN THE KINGDOM OF GOD. NOT FOR NOTORIETY'S SAKE

BUT FOR THE SAKE OF GOD'S PLANS AND PURPOSES;

FOR THE SAKE OF THE KINGDOM.

DARE TO BELIEVE THAT GOD IS NO RESPECTER OF PERSONS

THAT IF YOU ARE WILLING, HE WILL REVEAL HIMSELF TO YOU.

HE WILL MANIFEST HIMSELF TO YOU IN A TANGIBLE WAY.

HE WILL MAKE HIMSELF REAL TO YOU.

John 14:21

The person who has My commandments and keeps them is the one who really loves Me; and whoever [really] loves Me will be loved by My Father, and I [too] will love him and will show (reveal, manifest) Myself to him. [I will let Myself be clearly seen by him and make Myself real to him.]

Daniel 11:32b

. . . . .BUT THE PEOPLE WHO KNOW THEIR GOD SHALL PROVE THEMSELVES STRONG AND SHALL STAND FIRM AND DO EXPLOITS [FOR GOD

KNOW THE LIVING GOD!

GO FORTH!!!

DO EXPLOITS FOR GOD

EXCELERATE ® 2006

**TO ACCELERATE TOWARD EXCELLENCY
AND ACCOMPLISHMENT OR PROGRESS
IN ANY GIVEN THING.**

FOR THE BUILDING OF THE KINGDOM
OF GOD

ABOUT THE AUTHOR

Velma Crow
Ordained and Licensed

Velma is an anointed, experienced conference speaker and teacher who flows in the Spirit often addressing issues with the skill of a trained surgeon with words of wisdom and words of knowledge, both on the corporate and individual levels. She is dedicated to assisting in the revealing of the Sons of God and establishing His Kingdom on earth.

Velma's heart is to be used in propagating knowledge of the Living God and life in the Spirit, establishing skillful and godly wisdom in those around her. Her messages draw you deep into intimacy with God and give you a hunger for that tangible relationship with His ever-present Spirit. She has a heart for releasing others to love and live in wholeness and the fullness of their destiny.